1970s
LONDON
Discovering the Capital

A L E C   F O R S H A W

The
History
Press

Dedication

To Varinia Montero Perez (born 1974).

Acknowledgements

Thanks are due to my brother Roger, Mike Bruce, Geoffrey Pearce, Dick Makin, Richard Brockman and Anna Przylecka for unearthing photographs and allowing me to use them to enliven the text and book cover. I am grateful for the help of Philip Davies and Steve Hurst at English Heritage and for permission to use photographs from their collection. I am indebted to all those friends and colleagues who racked their brains and re-wound the tapes to recall many of the details so easily lost in the fug of increasing age and Middle Earth.

First published 2011

The History Press
The Mill, Brimscombe Port
Stroud, Gloucestershire, GL5 2QG
www.thehistorypress.co.uk

© Alec Forshaw, 2011

ISBN 978 0 7524 5691 1

Typesetting and origination by The History Press
Manufacturing managed by Jellyfish Print Solutions Ltd.
Printed in India

1970s
LONDON

CONTENTS

Like most of the population aged under twenty or over thirty who were either simply unaware of what was going on, or didn't like to ask, the Swinging Sixties largely passed me by. Following a sheltered childhood and a sequestered education at school and university in Cambridge, I was ready for a dose of the wider world. London in the early 1970s was where the lights seemed to shine the brightest.

In reality, London at that time was still a city struggling to find its post-war identity, a city full of declining industries, derelict docklands and run-down tenements, a townscape blighted by a rash of demonic motorway proposals, slum clearance schemes and undeveloped bomb-sites. The streets were still full of costermongers and greasy-spoon cafés, but enlivened by new ghettos of immigrants and student culture. Ideas of constraining traffic, conserving old buildings, recycling rubbish or promoting London as a 'world city' and tourist destination were in their infancy.

This was a decade which saw the three-day week, strikes over pay and conditions, the final anti-Vietnam protests, the Notting Hill riots and the winter of discontent. Bendy buses and congestion charging, Oyster cards and mobile phones, lottery numbers and cable television channels, laptops and private fitness clubs, gastro-pubs and sushi bars; these were all years away. It was a decade when many of the ideas of the 1960s were taken further and more extremely, and by a much larger number of people; a decade of excess which came to an end with Margaret Thatcher.

This book, a sequel to *Growing Up in Cambridge*, portrays the London of over thirty years ago as it appeared to a young man in his twenties, finding his feet, coming of age, stumbling across the sights, sounds and sensations of an extraordinary city. For him, these were the Serendipitous Seventies.

Bomb-sites awaiting development. (Mike Bruce)

❧ FINDING WORK ❧

Finding a job was not as easy as I had thought, or been led to believe, but to be fair I wasn't particularly sure what I wanted to do or was capable of doing. Temporary summer jobs picking fruit in Cambridgeshire orchards and working in Chivers' jam factory, and pre-Christmas Post Office sorting weren't promising prospects, and a degree in Geography, even with a decent 2:1 grade, wasn't exactly vocational.

Careers advice both at school in 1969 and at university in 1972 in Cambridge had been virtually zero. I thought, briefly, about applying to do a teaching diploma at the London Institute of Education in Malet Street, filled in the application form, and even went for an interview. I quickly decided against it. After seven years of cramming at school and three years of lectures, supervisions and exams at college, I had had enough of academia. Apart from a few of my friends who were tied into a seven-year haul at the School of Architecture or medical college, or off to do their law exams in London, 'getting a job' was the thing to do.

Someone had suggested the Government Communications Headquarters (GCHQ) as a possibility, so I duly went for two days of aptitude tests in their rather forbidding offices in Cheltenham in April 1972. Neither the town nor their premises appealed, and I turned down the job offer.

A colleague of my father working in the Great Ouse River Board had mentioned town planning as an opportunity. In the early 1970s, with barely a handful of private-sector consultancies, that meant local government. Off I plodded for interviews at Harlow New Town, with Frederick Gibberd, Stevenage New Town (a return train fare was 80p) and West Suffolk Planning Department in Bury St Edmunds, all unsuccessful.

Finally, in June, I was offered a job in Gillingham, Kent, and a month later, just after my twenty-first birthday, I started work as a trainee planner. The pay was £1,311 per annum, or after tax £81 per month, riches indeed after my annual student grant of £400. For four weeks I endured digs with a clucking elderly landlady in Abbey Road. Then I spied an advert in a shop window for a ground-floor bed-sit at No. 515 Canterbury Street, bang opposite the Town Hall and the creaking Portakabins where I worked. At £5 a week (plus coins in the slot for electricity), the rent was a quarter of my weekly wage, and I had to share a minimally equipped kitchen and a prehistoric bathroom with various odd characters who lived in other rooms in the house. But at least I could virtually roll out of bed into the office.

For all the benevolence of Raymond Williams, the Director of Planning, the motherliness of Mrs Brown, the dry wit and sagacity of my colleagues Paul Wood and John Dawson, I hated it. I was given the job of designating Tree Preservation Orders, which took me out and about and into the beautiful, rolling Kent countryside, and at least I learnt something about trees. Social life in Kent, however, was non-existent, apart from an invitation to join the local Rotary Club. Everyone, it seemed, went home promptly at five o'clock to their families in suburban houses on modern estates.

Fortunately, the 'trainee' part of the job title also meant that I was given day-release to do a professional planning course and sit for the Royal Town Planning Institute exams. I was offered places following interviews on the part-time courses at both the Polytechnic of North London and the Polytechnic of the South Bank, which had recently incorporated the old Brixton School of Building. I rejected the Polytechnic of North London because it was in a horrible building (undoubtedly true, and once voted the ugliest building in London) and in a dreary part of town which was difficult to get to. I wasn't to know that within five years I would be living barely five minutes' walk away! Instead, I started at the South Bank Poly in October 1972 in their passable premises in an old London County Council Board School in Battersea Park Road. The only

Majestic Battersea Power Station in its pomp, viewed across the river from Chelsea Embankment, 1974. (Geoffrey Pearce)

other option had been the Polytechnic of Central London (formerly the Regent Street Poly, and now the University of Westminster), where the course was run by the radical socialist Thom Blair.

On Thursdays I would take the fast train from Kent up to Victoria, swap onto a slow train stopping at the first station over the bridge, either Battersea Park or Queenstown Road, and then trudge along to college for my lectures. On the opposite side of Battersea Park Road, as far south as the main-line railway to Waterloo, the Victorian terraces had recently been replaced by ugly slab blocks of Council housing, now known as the Doddington and Rollo Estates. The new service roads had been given 'contemporary' names such as Strasburg Road and Francis Chichester Way. Sometimes in the lunch break with a group of fellow students, I ventured into the Grove, a modern Trumans' pub built for the estate, or the 1920s Eagle Tavern which alone had been spared the bulldozer. None of it inspired much confidence in town planning.

The main local landmark, then as now, was Battersea Power Station, still fully operational in 1972, with smoke billowing from the chimneys and mountainous piles of coal in the yards, extremely visible from the railway line. The power station too was still a relatively new building, and the B Station and fourth chimney had only been completed in 1955. While the 1930s A Station was closed in 1975, Battersea didn't finally stop working until 1983, after fifty years of generating electricity for London.

Riverside power stations were regarded in the early 1970s as a perfectly acceptable and normal part of London life, neither satanic nor iconic. The older Lots Road Power Station on the other side of the river at Chelsea generated electricity for the Underground throughout the 1970s. The oil-fired Bankside Power Station, opposite St Paul's Cathedral, was an even more recent building than Battersea, opened in 1963, and it operated until 1981. Nobody then was thinking about galleries of modern art or the problem of what to do with the leviathan that was Battersea.

After the intellectual rigours of my university degree, the part-time planning course was dull, little more than memorising lots of 'facts' and regurgitating the odd essay. Although the Polytechnic held its own exams for a diploma, I also had to sit the Royal Town Planning Institute's own professional exams. These were held in the University of London's examination halls in Taviton Street and Queen Square, Bloomsbury, depressingly huge rooms crammed with hundreds of child-sized desks and nervous students. Entrants were seated alphabetically and I never knew any of my neighbours. One was a man, old enough to be my father, called Fordham who asked me where I was from. He said he had come up from Devon and, bemoaning the 35 per cent failure rate, confessed that this was the twenty-third time he'd sat the exam. Thankfully I passed everything first time. Having completed Parts I, II, III and IV, I never wanted to do another exam again in my life.

Coming up to college in London for the day was fine and dandy and a chance to do something with friends in the evening. The worst thing was having to travel back later to Kent to work the following day. I longed to be in London permanently. Fortunately, I didn't have to wait too long.

∽ HARROW AND WEALDSTONE ∽

Harrow perhaps wasn't my number one choice for a job in London. Indeed, the London Borough of Harrow had officially only been part of London since 1965, when the former Urban District Council and Municipal Borough had been transferred from the old county of Middlesex to the newly established Greater London and it still retained its old Middlesex postal address. Harrow had been the only one of the thirty-two new London Boroughs to retain its previous administrative boundaries completely unchanged. All the others involved mergers of small Metropolitan Boroughs or other boundary adjustments. Perhaps that explained the apparent stability of the place.

Having failed to get a job in Islington in April 1973, and with little else being advertised, I accepted Harrow's offer of a job as an Assistant Planning Officer in July. Before the interview I'd never actually been to or through Harrow. I'd never really twigged where Harrow School, as in Eton vs Harrow cricket matches and their most famous pupil, Winston Churchill, actually was.

After the huts and sheds of Kent, the new Civic Centre of the London Borough of Harrow was impressively grand; a six-storey, free-standing block, square in plan and with a smaller cube attached which was the Council Chamber, all set in a flat sea of tarmac car parking. The building was only a year old, having been completed in 1972, and I probably saw it at its gleaming best. Subsequent architectural critics were less kind; 'heavy-handed vertical and horizontal rhythms and clumsy projecting panels' was how *The Buildings of England* described it in 1991. Nevertheless, the views out from my office on the fourth floor, north over the rooftops of Wealdstone and south to the trees and spire of St Mary's Church on the hill, were engaging.

I was allocated to the Local Plans team and the friendly chap who'd interviewed me became my amiable boss. Brian was semi-local and although he now lived and commuted in from Hemel Hempstead, he knew the area like the back of his hand. He and his colleague Jack, a northerner who'd moved down south from Louth in Lincolnshire, were both keen to make trips out of the office and equally willing to take me along too.

Although it wasn't by any means the biggest of the outer London Boroughs it was still a vast area, including Pinner, Stanmore, Canons Park, Hatch End and Kenton, as well as North,

Harrow Civic
Centre, 1974.
(Author's
Collection)

South, West and Central Harrow, Harrow Weald and, of course, Harrow-on-the-Hill. With over
210,000 residents it was twice the size of Cambridge, my home town.

The main immediate task at hand was preparing plans for the future development and
'improvement' of Harrow town centre and Wealdstone, which appeared to consist primarily of
highway engineers' proposals for building new relief roads and bypasses to serve multi-storey
car parks and new shopping malls. The same, no doubt, was going on in planning departments
all over the country.

Wealdstone was in reality a very mundane local shopping centre, straggling along its
north-south High Street, off which ran a series of east-west side streets lined with late Victorian
terraces and small factories. Major manufacturing industries dominated the area, with the giant
Kodak factory employing 4,700 people, HMSO print works another 1,000, Winsor & Newton
paints and Hamilton's Brush Co. a further 900, and Whitefriars Glass over 300. Most of these
workers lived in those humble, late Victorian terraces. The narrow curving road bridge over
the railway line by Harrow and Wealdstone Station was a bottleneck. Beside it and just beyond
the edge of the office car park, the Railway Station Hotel had seen better days and was not the
place to go to celebrate, or in fact to go at all.

The Civic Centre had a subsidised staff canteen, with main meals costing 20p and puddings 5p.
But with ready access to a car, and a laissez-faire regime of timekeeping, trips out to the remoter
parts of the Borough were a lot more fun. There was always the excuse of 'needing to see something'
on the way. The Queen's Head or the Victory in Pinner High Street were popular destinations, but
best was the Case Is Altered public house in Old Redding, up the hill at Harrow Weald. It seemed a
strange name for a pub, but someone said it was a corruption of 'Casa Alta', which soldiers returning
from the Napoleonic peninsula wars had called it. It was certainly a 'high house', with fine views
from the back garden to the south. On the north side of Old Redding were the overgrown grounds
of Grimsdyke, the extravagant Norman Shaw house where W.S. Gilbert (of Gilbert and Sullivan)
had lived and died while heroically saving someone from drowning in the garden pond.

The picturesque half-timbered Old English-style house had been used for twenty-five years
as a tuberculosis clinic and then a location for films such as *The Prime of Miss Jean Brodie*,
Ronnie Barker's *Futtocks End*, and a host of Vincent Price and Boris Karloff horror films.

John Betjeman had featured Grimsdyke in his 1973 *Metro-Land* film for the BBC. By then the house was experiencing a roller-coaster ride as a hotel, and in 1974 there were big signs in red letters on the padlocked gates saying 'DANGER: KEEP OUT'.

Many of Harrow's grand country houses had already been lost, and in the 1970s nobody really knew what to do with those that were left. I did manage to get inside Bentley Priory, the magnificent eighteenth-century house remodelled by Sir John Soane, which also had been the headquarters of the RAF Fighter Command during the war and their nerve-centre during the Battle of Britain. This too enjoyed a fabulous panorama from its terraces and lawns towards the south. After years of neglect by the Ministry of Defence, an outbreak of dry rot caused the closure of the mess building in March 1975 and the embarrassing relocation of the Summer Ball, attended by the Queen Mother, into a temporary marquee. It caused quite a fuss, and instigated a fundraising campaign to 'Save the Priory'. I was lucky to see it then, because a disastrous fire in 1979 destroyed much of the original internal fabric.

When I started work I had taken lodgings in a dreary bed-sit in Welldon Crescent, halfway between the Civic Centre and central Harrow. The shopping centre in those days had little to commend it. The National Coal Board, inexplicably, had their headquarters in Lyon Road (not many coalmines in Harrow) in the prosaically named Coal House, one of a series of dull 1960s slabs built on stilts with cars parked underneath, and there were offices of local estate agents and solicitors. It was dead in the evening.

The miners' strike in December 1973 (when they rejected a 13 per cent pay offer) and the three-day week which was imposed by the government in January 1974 propelled the NCB into the news, and boosted the sale of candles. The rationing of electricity and petrol, triggered by the quadrupling of oil prices by Arab countries, affected all commercial operations including the Civic Centre. There was humorous talk about the government banning the sale or use of various luxury items such as hedge-trimmers and hostess trolleys, even restricting households to heating only one room. Edward Heath apparently vetoed any mention of the troubles by

Winsor & Newton's factory, 1973. (Author's Collection)

the Queen in her Christmas message. For me, as someone with little responsibility, it all seemed rather exciting at the time, even disappointing when the matter was resolved and we all went back to working five days a week in early March.

Harrow-on-the-Hill offered more congenial surroundings and attractions such as the Castle and North Star pubs and the King's Head Hotel. I even managed to wangle my way into using the school squash courts. It was the only contact I ever had with the school. Although they owned a swathe of property in the village, they were singularly self-contained and seemed to bother no one, and vice versa. There was something rather unreal about this hilltop enclave, when at the foot of the slopes beyond the playing fields and rugby posts there stretched mile upon mile of suburbia in every direction.

The decision in 1974 to embark on appraisals and designations of conservation areas gave an added excuse to spend time in Harrow-on-the-Hill, Stanmore and Pinner. At that time conservation areas were a relatively new invention (introduced by the 1967 Civic Amenities Act), and certainly a novelty for the London Borough of Harrow. The instruction had filtered down from the Director of Development and Technical Services. Geoffrey Foxley was an architect with a reputation for gruffness, whose spacious office was, predictably, on the top floor. Although we sometimes saw him in the lift, I was too junior to have any direct contact. I went up to the eyrie only once, on my last day, mumbling my thanks before rushing off to the King's Head for farewell drinks. After wading my way through the pints stacked up on the table, I have no idea how I got home. Presumably I didn't drive.

Harrow gave me a toehold in London, but almost from the start I'd realised that the suburbs wasn't the bit of London where I really wanted to be. I had enjoyed the conservation area work, and it gave me a taste for architectural detail and vernacular building styles. Coupled with a pay rise which took my salary to the heady heights of £2,000, it didn't seem too bad a way to earn a living, but when I was offered a job in inner London I jumped at it.

∽ HENDON ∽

My commencement of work in Harrow happily coincided with the arrival in London of various friends who, unlike me, had done a year out between school and university, and had therefore only just graduated but were now being lured for a variety of reasons to London. During my year treading water in Kent, and doing my part-time course in Battersea, I had spent most weekends back in Cambridge, attracted by the prospect of seeing my girlfriend, drinking in the old haunts of college bars and using the parental washing machine. Hitchhiking was still a common and accepted activity, although it was never easy getting out of London. Normally I would get a bus out to Apex Corner on the A1 or the train to Turkey Street on the Great Cambridge Road in Enfield, where it was easier to thumb a lift.

That summer I had also bought a car, on a tip-off from someone in the Gillingham office, at an auction held by the Kent County Constabulary. My acquisition was an immaculate light blue Morris Minor which had been a police 'Panda' car, its flashing light on the roof replaced by a small, round rubber plug. It was only two years old, and at £100 an absolute bargain; OPM 409F, or 'Opum Funf' as it became known, certainly made it easier to get around.

Three friends from Corpus Christi College in Cambridge, Pete, Dave and Robin, had found a substantial five-bedroom house to rent in Hendon and invited me and a girl called Marcia to fill up the space. Although Hendon wasn't exactly close to Harrow, it seemed to be roughly on the same latitude and reasonably close, now that I was armed with my new car.

Hendon had been one of those amorphous bits of outer London which we'd driven through in the 1960s on family outings from Cambridge whenever we were aiming for the west side of London. The square clock tower of the Blue Star garage and the adjacent Vernon Flats at the top of Finchley Road had always marked the real start of London, when suddenly the buildings got bigger, but Apex Corner, Mill Hill Broadway, Henly's Corner and Hendon Central had been minor blips on the way. Over the years we'd seen the road improved and widened, most noticeably in 1965 by the Brent Cross flyover with its three levels of 'spaghetti' spanning the North Circular.

Watford Way, as the main road was known, had been driven through in 1927 and up the hill from Hendon Central crossed a much older east-west road, the Burroughs. Apparently several old houses had been demolished and an ancient pond filled in to create the traffic-light junction, leaving several cedars and a new war memorial stranded in the central reservation. Little did I know that I would end up, in my first proper place to live in London, right beside this thundering arterial road.

The Burroughs was originally one of several detached hamlets which occupied the high ground of Hendon parish. Ivy House, No. 13, was part of the small group of early eighteenth-century houses which had survived the road builders on the north side, and with its pretty, projecting curved bay at the front was the tallest and seemingly narrowest of the group. In fact, it was bigger and deeper than it looked because at the rear a spacious farmhouse kitchen wrapped sideways around the back of No. 15 next door. The house had a basement, accessible only by ladder, pitch-dark and damp, front and rear living rooms on the ground floor, two bedrooms on the first floor and three in the attic, with a half-landing bathroom at the back off the stairs. I had the smallest front attic room, with a little round-arched timber casement window, gently rotting away, but at least we all had the luxury of our own rooms. In 1973 it was all in a fairly dilapidated condition and the kitchen was infested with mice, which would jump out of the drawers in the Welsh dresser. The garden at the back was long and thin, but truncated by the Watford Way, and so noisy that it was unusable for any sort of pleasurable purpose. The solitary gnarled apple tree seemed twisted in protest at the road.

The owner, or absentee landlord, was a man called Kleinman who was reputed to own other houses nearby. I never met him at the time, and probably assumed he lived in Golders Green, but when some years later, completely by chance, I met his musical daughter it transpired that he lived in a beautiful house in Highbury Terrace, Islington. Our rental agreement was on a very short tenure. Rumour had it that Kleinman wanted to redevelop and build in the back garden, which is what eventually happened.

Either side of our house were grander houses, but equally run down, and next door was a single-storey antiques shop which almost always seemed to be closed. Beyond that was a vacant and unfenced site, where I parked my car.

In 1973 public transport from Hendon to Harrow was impossible without going into and back out of central London, with few of the cross-country buses which exist now in the suburbs. It was about seven miles by car, an uninspiring journey through the suburban dystopia of Colindale, Kingsbury and Kenton. On Christmas Eve 1973, while parked on the pavement outside the house to load up my bags and presents before the journey back to Cambridge, and having run inside for one last thing, the car was stolen. A solemn and dispirited Yuletide was followed by several gruelling weeks of cycling fourteen miles every day to and from Harrow, but in mid-January the car was found abandoned on a verge in Hertfordshire. The police said it had been used as a getaway car, which sounded unlikely, unless the thieves thought that a lack of speed was compensated by its inconspicuous appearance.

Social life in Ivy House focused on the local pubs. Many of our evenings were spent in the White Bear, just a few yards east along the Burroughs. This one-time country inn had

The Burroughs, with Ivy House in the centre, 1973. (Author's Collection)

been rebuilt in 1932 in half-timbered Tudorbethan style, and its main attraction, apart from its proximity to the house, was the bar-billiard table which had taken over from college table football as our new communal compulsive leisure activity.

Sometimes we ventured further along the Burroughs, past the rather pompous neo-Renaissance Hendon Town Hall, the Edwardian fire station, the neo-Baroque public library and the dour technical college (now part of Middlesex University), until we turned into Church End. Ignoring the Chequers pub we walked on, round the next bend, until we reached the Greyhound. This truly had the appearance of a country pub, nestled beside the medieval St Mary's Church and the old village core of Hendon.

The Greyhound also sold real ale. In 1973, when fizzy keg beer was seemingly everywhere, including the White Bear and the Chequers, this was our holy grail. The downside of the Greyhound was that it was the closest decent pub to the Metropolitan Police Training College in Aerodrome Road, and was all too frequently packed with their raw recruits, a few of whom always seemed to be looking for a fight. That year the college was being considerably and hideously extended, and in May 1974, when Robert Peel's statue (relocated from Cheapside) was unveiled by the Queen, it was renamed the Peel Centre School.

Conveniently near our house on the Burroughs was a small parade of shops, which included a newsagent, Cobb's butchers, Barnet greengrocers, Brampton general stores, and Burroughs Bakery, soon to close. Down the hill from the Burroughs was Hendon Central, a circus of rather bland neo-Georgian red-brown brick buildings. There was a small Woolworth's, a True-form shoe shop and a Jewish deli, nothing like as fancy as Golders Green, but good enough for our cheese-on-toast needs. The main road, no doubt, brought passing trade to the Wimpy bar, the State Chinese restaurant and Kentucky Fried Chicken, branches of which had sprung up all over London in the early '70s. Their takeaway nuggets still had a certain novelty attraction. There was also a grubby cinema where in March 1974 I saw the scary double bill of *Don't Look Now* and *The Wicker Man*, both to become cult films.

Just half a mile to the south, construction had started on the Brent Cross Shopping Centre. Heralded as the first stand-alone shopping mall in the United Kingdom, there was some excitement about the new flagship stores of John Lewis and Fenwicks, but there was also apprehension among Hendon's local shopkeepers about the loss of trade. Brent Cross, when it finally opened in 1976, was in reality entirely geared towards the car, poorly served by bus and virtually inaccessible by foot, should anyone have been mad enough to try. Thirty-four years later there is now a scheme to make it even bigger, attracting an extra 29,000 vehicles a day. Not many lessons have been learnt.

In the event, Brent Cross arrived too late for my Hendon days. In July 1974, during a party at the house when thirty people were packed into the rear ground-floor room, it displayed what an engineer might call structural distress. The next day some workmen arrived and installed scaffolding props and sealed off the rear room. Rather abruptly we were asked to leave to find somewhere else to live.

✎ HAMPSTEAD ✎

The nearest place with real charm and character easily reached from Hendon was Hampstead, just three stops from Hendon Central down the Edgware branch of the Northern Line. Many times we spent merry evenings in one or more of the several excellent pubs in Hampstead village.

In the 1970s Hampstead still retained some of its genuine Bohemian and artistic flavour and had not as yet been overrun by the moneyed classes or tourists. Pubs such as the Rosslyn Arms on Rosslyn Hill, where my thespian uncle had taken me as an adolescent to sample his favourite tipple of scrumpy from the wooden barrel, was still a basic locals' local: unpretentious, scruffy, cheap and friendly. There were still small shops selling milk, bread, cigarettes and newspapers, rather than designer clothes and jewellery.

Our favourite hostelry for good beer was the Flask, tucked away behind the High Street and tube station on Flask Walk. I had been introduced to this splendid place by my school friend Jonny, who was now living in Goldhurst Terrace, not a million miles away just the other side of the Finchley Road up from Swiss Cottage, behind John Barnes, which was still then a department store. While working in Kent and doing my day-release course in Battersea, we'd sometimes meet up in the evening and occasionally I'd stayed on his floor overnight. The Flask was well worth the twenty minute hike up Fitzjohn's Avenue. It was a famous Mecca for North London musicians and theatricals, mainly brass players, but also well-known regulars such as the cellist Dougie Cummings. The small public bar became packed later on in the evening as players arrived in dinner jackets with their instrument cases, having finished shows or concerts in the West End. Late arrivals raced to quaff down enough pints of Young's to slake their thirst before closing time.

Several other Hampstead pubs offered excellent beer. The Wells Tavern in Well Walk, just along from John Constable's house, was more comfortable and relaxed than the Flask, and sold Wethered's beer, still then being brewed in Marlow, Buckinghamshire, although it had been taken over by Whitbread. The Holly Bush in Holly Mount and the Horse and Groom on Heath Street were other options, the former cosy and quaint with its little rooms and timber panelling, the latter more chintzy and raucous facing the main road.

The future of beer making and the availability of a good pint was a major topic of conversation. The Campaign for Real Ale (CAMRA), or the Revitalisation of Ale as it was originally intended, had been founded in 1971 by Michael Hardman and three drinking companions. CAMRA's membership mushroomed and in 1974 the first *Good Beer Guide* was published. CAMRA also ventured into pub ownership and bought the Nag's Head, opposite the Horse and Groom in Heath Street. This had been a perfectly good and unassuming

The Flask in Hampstead, 1974.
(Author's Collection)

McMullens pub, selling their pleasant AK bitter. Now suddenly it boasted an exotic range of beers from outside London and became packed with large bellies and loud voices. Similar ventures elsewhere proved less successful, and by 1981 the Nag's Head was sold off to pay for debts elsewhere, eventually to become an All Bar One, and today an estate agent.

Hampstead also had its heath, which I'd known in part as a child, accompanying my uncle when he walked his dog. Now I got to know it more thoroughly, including those less-frequented bits north of Spaniards Road and behind Jack Straw's Castle. Most beguiling were the overgrown ramparts of The Hill, the former mansion and grounds of Viscount Leverhulme. Its post-war use as part of Manor House Hospital had ceased and in the 1970s the huge house lay empty and neglected. Perched above the wild woods below, the elevated gardens were a fairyland fantasy of Edwardian grandeur, arcades of crumbling red brick and decaying pergolas smothered in roses, clematis and ivy. From the terraces there were stunning sunset views across West Heath over the canopy of birch and alder away to the distant cone and pointed spire of Harrow-on-the-Hill. Not until the Corporation of London eventually took over the heath from the defunct Greater London Council (GLC) in 1989 were the gardens restored, and the house converted to flats.

In contrast to these sylvan delights there was 'Appy 'Ampstead Fair at Easter and Whitsun when the level areas near the Vale of Health and the car park at the bottom end of East Heath Road were full of stalls and pleasure rides, candyfloss and cockney characters. All the nearby pubs were packed, especially the Freemasons Arms on the corner with Downshire Hill. 'Mind your bags and watch your pockets' were wise words.

In 1971 my older brother Roger had come to London to do a PhD at University College. He had moved into a miniscule bed-sit in Holmdale Road, West Hampstead, one of the maze of little streets off the west side of West End Lane, behind the shops and Iverson Road library, unassuming but convenient. The BBC reporter Martin Bell lived opposite, but nobody then would have guessed that he would become famous as an independent MP and 'the man in the white suit'.

My brother's research subject was in electronics (the development of read-only memory devices for a Pattern Recognition machine), and his knowledge and enthusiasm was vigorously applied in practical terms with gadgets and mechanisms, operated remotely by telephone, for closing the curtains, putting on the heating, and sensor mats for detecting whether his snooping landlord had come into his room while he was out. His summer social life often revolved around Hampstead Heath, conveniently with a girlfriend living in Wildwood Road overlooking the Sandy Heath. Convivial picnics at Kenwood concerts and kite-flying on Sunday mornings on Parliament Hill were regular events. I, too, by then had met a new girlfriend who was living in a smart pad in Willow Road, not far from Goldfinger's modernist house. Suddenly, Hampstead seemed to be the centre of the world, or, at any rate, where I wanted to be.

When occupancy of the Hendon house came to its sudden and calamitous end, Hampstead seemed the obvious place to look for somewhere else to live. After much scouring of the

A walk in the woods; the author, Robin and Tim. (Geoffrey Pearce)

West Hampstead Station, part of British Rail Midland Region, 1974. (Roger Forshaw)

Evening Standard, Robin and I answered an address in Heath Drive, a wide tree-lined avenue off Finchley Road. The flat on offer was apparently self-contained, on the ground floor of a huge Edwardian house, lived in by a middle-aged lady with a thick Central European accent. She said she was a psychiatrist, and would charge us £15 a week each. It seemed a lot, but after inhaling a deep breath, we resolved to take it. Maybe that's what you had to pay to live in Hampstead.

Within two days it turned out that the dear lady was mad, and far from the flat being self-contained, she seemed to be a continual and intolerable presence. She announced that she hated music and would not allow any musical instruments to be played, neither of which suited Robin or me. We decided there and then to leave. Robin retreated back to Nottingham to stay with his parents; I loaded everything I had (fortunately not very much) into my Morris Minor.

My brother's tiny bed-sit in Holmdale Road was an immediate refuge, but not an ideal long-term solution. Jonny's living-room carpet in his more spacious flat in Goldhurst Terrace had the attraction of late-night listening to Jonny's impressive collection of LPs, rich in Mahler, Messiaen and Duke Ellington, but crashing out and kipping on other people's floors was an imposition and didn't go down that well with his trombonist flatmates. For about a month I lived in my car. There was a shower in the squash courts at Harrow, and at least there was the office to go to during the day. For most of August I was away in Austria, Cornwall and then Ibiza, all trips involving playing the bassoon in various orchestras. Nevertheless, it was an uncomfortable time, when the prospects for the subtitle of this book might have been 'From Scholar to Squalor'.

I had got to know Swiss Cottage and Chalk Farm in the 1960s during visits to London to see my actor uncle, John. He lived in Ainger Road, a quiet street of grubby mid-Victorian terraces close to Primrose Hill. Most of Chalk Farm was black with soot from the smoke in the railway cutting. Although the steam engines had been replaced by diesels in the early 1970s, not much else had changed.

Now that I was living in London, I occasionally went round to visit John in his untidy top-floor flat. The piles of half-read scripts, the rudimentary kitchen piled with dirty washing-up, and the glacial shared lavatory on the stairs' landing were just the same, but it all now seemed scruffier and less romantic than I remembered as a wide-eyed teenager. His dog, Mac, was older now, but still barked incessantly. We would go out to eat at Marine Ices on Chalk Farm Road or Manna, round the corner in Erskine Road. This had opened in 1966 as a vegetarian restaurant and in 1973 it was cheap and cheerful, little more than a local café, but the food was filling and wholesome. Today it claims to be the oldest survivor of its type in the UK.

By now my uncle was increasingly worried by threats of redevelopment in the area. All the talk was of proposals for road building, and in particular the notorious Ringway One, which was being promoted by the GLC. This was threatening much of the Chalk Farm and Swiss Cottage area. Dozens of substantial semi-detached Victorian houses in King Henry's Road and Adelaide Road were vacant and boarded up, screened off from the street by corrugated iron, gardens full of rampant buddleia. The acquisition of property had been going on for years, and in anticipation of the road scheme new high-rise housing blocks were under construction on the north side of Adelaide Road, being given fanciful and irrelevant names such as Dorney, Bray, Burnham and Taplow. Even at the time of their construction they seemed inappropriate and ugly stumps, completely at odds with the established character of Primrose Hill or Belsize Park. While the 1960s mania for high-rise was subsiding, there was now an appetite for large-scale low-rise. The Alexandra Road Estate, built between 1972 and 1978, might well have been a response by the architect Neave Brown to the hideous twenty-storey towers of the Abbey Road Estate, but its raw concrete aroused huge hostility during its construction. At least Neave Brown did the honourable, and very rare, thing of actually living on the estate he had designed, and campaigning tirelessly for its regular maintenance.

The concern was that the fever for redevelopment would spread south to Chalk Farm itself. My uncle began to think about moving out of London. His absentee landlord would do nothing to improve the house, not even redecorate the peeling brown paint on the windows, perhaps not surprising given the seeming probability of compulsory purchase.

At Swiss Cottage, a huge area immediately north of Basil Spence's 1960s library and swimming pool had been cleared and this became the focus of more radical community activity. Friends of the Earth, founded in California in 1969, had established a foothold in London in 1971 and one of the first local branches was Camden FOE. My brother and some of his chums became involved with their activities, most notably in what were then revolutionary ideas of paper and glass recycling. I sometimes went along to help or join in. On Saturdays a depot was set up, together with several stalls on the waste ground, and in one of the empty shops nearby my brother helped run a bicycle-repair workshop, offering to fix things for free or a donation to the cause. In a shop in Winchester Road, just along from the spit-and-sawdust Winchester Arms pub, a friendly community café was run by a jolly lady called Rosa, the window full of posters and small ads.

Friends of the Earth attracted a motley collection of enthusiastic individuals, a few cranks and crackpots, but mainly young people who wanted to do something to reverse the seemingly

Alexandra Road housing estate under construction next to the Euston railway line, 1973. (Richard Brockman)

unstoppable tide of waste and destruction. Even though most of the proceeds from the newspaper recycling were spent on printing leaflets and postage for their various campaigns, it seemed worthwhile. This was, after all, the very beginning of any sort of public awareness of environmental issues, and nobody then had even begun to think about the possibility of global warming. At the time there seemed to be more pressing issues, hence campaigns such as 'Save the Whale' and 'Babies against the Bomb'. For lots of people it really seemed to matter that the Earth was being polluted and over-populated. Little stickers saying 'Population is your Baby' were put up everywhere. On the political front, Tony Whittaker founded the People's Party in 1973, re-launched as the Ecology Party in 1975 (and eventually renamed the Green Party in 1990).

The bike-repair enterprise was very popular and one of my brother's co-workers, Errol Drew, saw the commercial potential. In 1978 he left a dull job in the Prudential and set up his own shop, Beta Bikes, at No. 275 West End Lane, a stone's throw from my brother's flat. Errol later emigrated to the USA and established a chain of cycle retail stores called Freewheel, but the bike shop in West End Lane is still there, now the Cycle Surgery.

Camden Lock was similarly blighted by the GLC motorway, even though the new road and its intersections with local 'feeder' roads were proposed to be elevated, like Westway. For decades after the war the Regent's Canal had become a forgotten backwater. By the early 1970s, any canal-side industry and wharves that had withstood competition from road and rail freight was in terminal decline. On the north side of Camden Lock Dingwall's timber yard and the surrounding warehousing lay empty. In 1972 a group of young entrepreneurs took a short lease from the British Waterways Board and sublet some of the ramshackle old buildings on very cheap rents. Among the first tenants were five female students of the Hornsey College of

Art, who were budding jewellers. The workshops soon became a colony for potters, painters, cabinet-makers, leather-workers and a host of other creative trades. Even national newspapers and their first colour supplements began to take note.

By March 1974 the motorway blight had been lifted and a craft market started on the cobbled open ground north of the canal bridge, initially quite a small and sedate affair just

The Aerated Bread Co. (ABC) bakery still going strong in 1973, later pulled down for Sainsbury's supermarket. (English Heritage)

My brother Roger at the bicycle workshop, Swiss Cottage, 1973. (Roger Forshaw)

on Saturday afternoons, hardly larger than the little market which had set up on the waste land at Swiss Cottage. At Camden Lock, the market thrived and grew like Topsy. Looking at Chalk Farm Road and Camden High Street north of the tube station today, it is not easy to recall that thirty-five years ago it was just an ordinary street of small local shops and a few chains such as Littlewoods, where ladies bought net curtains. Inverness Street had a lively little daily market with cockney stallholders selling fruit and veg, cheap clothes and household goods at knock-down prices. Not until the 1980s did Nicholas Grimshaw's new Sainsbury's supermarket arrive to steal the trade from the local shops and stallholders. The grim backside of Grimshaw's store on Kentish Town Road replaced the Art Deco tiles of the ABC Bakery.

The elegant early Victorian terraces in side streets such as Albert Street, Arlington Road and Gloucester Crescent were already showing signs of being a smart address and attracting the likes of George Melly, Jonathan Miller and Alan Bennett. Successful architectural practices were moving into backstreet premises. Sheppard Robson's ingenious conversion in 1976 of empty industrial buildings around an irregular courtyard off Parkway was pioneering (and a stunning venue for office parties).

Camden Lock became a place to go and hang out on Saturdays, and by 1976 on Sundays too. Smart restaurants opened such as Lock Stock and Barrel and Le Routier. One of the old narrow boats, the *Jenny Wren*, was done up to offer canal trips.

Before the overwhelming invasion of knick-knacks, fast food, gothic clothes shops and mass tourism, Camden Town had an edginess, at the bow-wave of fashion. For London it became in the 1970s what the King's Road had been in the '60s.

Camden Town was where I ate my first Greek food. Cosy tavernas such as Andy's and Moditi's (now renamed Daphne), still side-by-side in Bayham Street, Paphos in Pratt Street,

Camden Lock. (Theo Bergström)

Nontas in the High Street and Koritsas in Kentish Town Road offered a glimpse, real or imagined, of a Greek paradise, in surroundings adorned with swirling Artex plaster and real or plastic vines. Here, for the first time, I ate hummus and feta cheese, sheftalia and dolmades, all washed down with rough retsina wine.

The pubs were a mixed bag. The four famous Victorian 'castle' pubs, the Windsor, the Dublin, the Edinburgh and the Caernarvon, had supposedly been named as a response to the ethnic variety of Camden Town. It seemed to me as though the Irish had a strong foothold in them all. The Spread Eagle in Parkway offered the best Young's beer, and was still divided into little snugs and parlours, each with their own regulars. The Hawley Arms in Castlehaven Road was closest to the Camden Lock Market. In 1976 this was just a basic local, with none of the trendiness which came with clientele such as Amy Winehouse and Pete Doherty. Indeed, they hadn't even been born.

The Roundhouse up at Chalk Farm had already become an iconic music venue in the 1960s for an eclectic mix of concerts, whether pop, jazz or classical. Jimi Hendrix, Pink Floyd, the Doors and Fairport Convention all played there. *Oh! Calcutta!* caused something of a stir when it was staged in 1970. It was also used for avant-garde groups, such as Peter Maxwell Davies' Fires of London who performed his *Eight Songs for a Mad King*. Despite the success of shows by Motörhead and Kraftwerk, and by The Ramones, whose concert in July 1976 was said to have started the UK punk-rock movement, the Roundhouse struggled financially. The walls inside and out were still caked black from its days as an engine shed, the heating was non-existent and the ablutionary facilities Spartan. Increasingly in debt despite GLC subsidies it struggled on, but eventually it closed in 1983 to be followed by a decade of darkness.

New venues such as the Electric Ballroom and the Music Machine (later the Camden Palace and now Koko) opened in 1977, the latter in the opulent surroundings of the Royal Camden Theatre. They thrived, helped by the closure of the Rainbow at Finsbury Park, but in doing so perhaps contributed also to the demise of the Roundhouse.

With the abandonment of the motorway proposals, the streets of Primrose Hill and Chalk Farm were spared. But instead of the bulldozer and concrete mixer there were now new socially motivated ideas for improving housing conditions, led by the local authorities. In Ainger Road, my uncle's landlord was being bought out by Camden Council so that the house could be refurbished and converted into properly self-contained flats, all with their own bathrooms. Not fancying the offer of being re-housed in a modern municipal block 'somewhere in Camden', John and his partner, Ernest, decided in 1977 to move to Hove, not the first or last couple with an artistic bent to encamp in the Brighton area. He was keen that I should have his grand piano, a big pre-First World War Bechstein, with worn-out hammers and ineffectual dampers. I had nowhere to put it, and I couldn't find anyone else who did. I even asked Hecksher's, the piano parts shop in Bayham Street, if they'd be interested in having it for spares. In the end John took it with him, laden with decades of Camden Town dust.

◈ SOMERS TOWN AND FITZROVIA ◈

South of Mornington Crescent the townscape seemed bleaker and more fragmented. Even the huge hulk of Greater London House (formerly the Carreras cigarette factory) had been stripped bare of its Art Deco Egyptian details and was minimally occupied. I did stay, for one night only in July 1972 before I had a base in London, in one of the Regency villas in Park Village East. Pretty though Nash's stucco and fretwork filigree was, the house faced the chasm of the Euston railway cutting, protected by a long, high red-brick wall. Even then most of the stone orbs on top of the pillars had fallen off. Across the cutting were the three stumpy towers of the 1960s Ampthill Square Estate, and further south the villas gave way to gaunt post-war Council estates.

Dominating this whole area was the thirty-six storey, 124m-high Euston Tower, finished and opened in 1973. Most people, including my uncle who had seen its daily progress walking his dog on Primrose Hill, considered the Euston Centre an alien and shocking insertion into the London skyline and into the West End in particular, the result of a long and sordid property speculation in the 1960s by the Levy brothers, all wrapped up in the construction of the Tottenham Court Road underpass and the widening of Euston Road. Capital Radio was launched there in October 1973, just one week after LBC Radio, occupying the ground and first floor, not the top as they sometimes claimed. They didn't, actually, have great views across London. The four-square ugliness of the Euston Tower also spoilt views of the elegant and stylishly slim Post Office Tower nearby. Since 1965 this had become a popular new London landmark, even though they had to close the revolving restaurant at the top after a Provisional IRA bomb explosion in 1971. Further east along Euston Road, the 1960s had done their worst at Euston Station, tearing down the Euston Arch and preparing the way for Seifert's three cheerless office blocks, built from 1974 to 1978.

Between Euston Station and Euston Tower lay Tolmers Square, and a huge planning battle. I had heard about this from some of the Swiss Cottage Friends of the Earth activists, who were interested that I was a trainee planner. Tolmers Square itself comprised solid 1850s houses, deliberately run down and neglected by the owners who were hell-bent on redevelopment for yet more offices. Many of the original tenants had been forced out, but were replaced by squatters who were determined to put up a fight.

Without any form of protection through listing, Tolmers Square didn't stand much of a chance. Even had it been a conservation area, which it wasn't, the controls over demolition were weak in the 1970s. The so-called compromise which was reached by Camden Council didn't save any of the buildings in Tolmers Square. What it did achieve was some replacement housing along Hampstead Road, rather than purely offices, and buildings substantially lower than the Euston Tower.

The new mirror-glass frontage to Euston Road, designed by Renton Howard Wood in 1975, was also arguably more interesting to look at than the bland, international style Sidney Kaye had adopted for the Euston Centre.

Mercifully the excessive and unnecessary widening of Hampstead Road had spared the east side. Here on the corner with Drummond Street, which had also been saved, I discovered Laurence Corner. It was a remarkable shop, ostensibly Army and Navy surplus clothing, but in reality an emporium and Aladdin's cave of fancy dress and accessories. For some people it was a shrine, because celebrities such as Barry White had been there. It was, allegedly, where the Beatles found their inspiration and the military uniforms to go with it for *Sergeant Pepper's Lonely Hearts Club Band*. For me it was the place to buy jackets, ex-naval pullovers, socks, balaclavas and woollen gloves, all made to survive the rigours of National Service, at ridiculously low prices. It seems incredible that when the owner, Victor Jamilly, died in 2007 his family couldn't find a buyer. Sixty years after it opened it simply closed (although his daughter has recently opened a successor at Camden Lock).

An additional good-value attraction in Drummond Street was the Bhel Poori House, then one of the cheapest vegetarian Indian restaurants in London. They offered 'eat-as-much-as-you-want' lunches for £1.

South of the Euston Road, Fitzrovia had a more genteel seediness and more gastronomic pleasures. In the mid-1970s the south side of Robert Adam's Fitzroy Square was still in ruins after the war, and its rebuilding by Rolfe Judd wasn't finished until 1980. Other small

Tolmers Square and the Euston Tower, 1973. (English Heritage)

bomb-sites were still sprinkled around the area, fenced off with corrugated iron plastered in posters and graffiti. The greatest concentration of restaurants was in Charlotte Street, where the most celebrated was Schmidt's delicatessen and restaurant. This was the last vestige of the German community which had settled north of Oxford Street in the late nineteenth century, and which was sometimes known then as 'Charlottenstrasse'. Schmidt's, at Nos 35-37, had opened in 1901 and arguably not a lot had changed since then. It was famous for its curt waiters and reasonable prices, staple middle-European main courses such as eisbein with sauerkraut or frankfurters with spaetzle. By 1976 the local German/Jewish community had long since relocated to Golders Green or Edgware, and society at large had no passion for such stolid fare. Schmidt's closed and lay empty for years afterwards.

More attractive was the cluster of Greek Cypriot tavernas, the New Kebab House, the Venus Kebab House, the Little Akropolis and, best of all, Anemos at No. 34. This became a regular venue for post-concert meals for anyone living north, on they way home from St John's Smith Square or the South Bank, and a favourite of the Young Publishers Association after their meetings. It usually lived up to its name, although I never experienced the plate-smashing for which I was once told the animated owner had a liking. In fact, I've never seen this happen in any Greek restaurant, and it always seemed a dubious myth, even for someone with shares in crockery.

Further north in Whitfield Street were two Indian restaurants, the Agra and the Diwan-I-Am, which specialised in tandoori and hot vindaloo curries. The brass players often went there. More sensitive souls and vegetarians went to the Hare Krishna in Hanway Street or, better still, the Mandeer at No. 21 Hanway Place, hard to find down poorly-lit basement stairs, but rewarded by exquisite tastes. Sadly it has long since closed.

Otherwise, Fitzrovia was still full of sweatshops and the rag trade. Two friends, Neil and Elspeth, half-American brother and sister, lived in a flat at No. 61 Goodge Street, above Clara's, a ladies' bonnet and hat-shape maker. I'd met Neil as a fellow bassoon player, and Elspeth was learning to tune pianos at the London College of Furniture. Downstairs, on the ground floor, Clara had given up the ghost but left behind a surreal collection of 1940s mannequins in the shop window. The One Tun pub was conveniently opposite, but Neil preferred the spit-and-sawdust of the Duke of York, tucked away round the corner in Charlotte Place. They heard about the demise of Schmidt's and made sure they acquired some of the monogrammed cutlery at the death.

⤟ BLOOMSBURY ⤠

The community struggles at Swiss Cottage and Tolmers Square against the seemingly inexorable and irresistible pressure from property developers made me realise that there were far more exciting and demanding issues in central London than I was experiencing in the sleepy suburban backwaters of Harrow Planning Department.

Bloomsbury was another area where major change was afoot, but here the perpetrators were mainly the university or the local authority. I had visited my brother's laboratory and faculty at the University College Department of Engineering in 1972, a ten-storey 1960s brick box with a main entrance onto Malet Place, not dissimilar to the equivalently bland buildings in Cambridge, but with more spectacular views from the roof. Dillons' bookshop was directly opposite on Torrington Place. Around the corner I had had an interview at the Institute of Education in Malet Street, an equally dull architectural experience.

The 'rape' of Bloomsbury had, of course, been going on for a long time, from at least the early 1930s, when the university had acquired and begun clearing away Georgian squares and terraces for new academic and institutional buildings. The loss of most of Woburn and Torrington Squares, together with the demolition of the Adelphi south of the Strand, had triggered the founding of the Georgian Group by those who were outraged by such wanton destruction, even though today, with hindsight, we might to have come to rather like some of the 1930s replacements, such as Charles Holden's Senate House.

The 1960s had seen some of the worst desecrations of Bloomsbury, such as the replacement of the resplendent Edwardian Imperial Hotel and the obliteration of the western end of Red Lion Square for the Proctor Street one-way system, but there were still many redevelopment projects in the pipeline or underway in the 1970s. The Brunswick Centre had been conceived in 1959, initially by Leslie Martin and Patrick Hodgkinson in partnership, but construction did not start until 1968 and was not finished until 1973, by then with just Hodgkinson in charge. Originally intended to extend northwards to Tavistock Place, its ambition was curtailed. An even greater 'mega-structure' was Denys Lasdun's new Institute of Education, occupying the whole of the west side of Bedford Way. This again had been planned in 1965 but was only completed in 1976. To many enlightened commentators, the external monolithic expression of horizontality and projecting service towers was considered stark and forbidding. Most people simply thought it was hideous. Lasdun's brutalism certainly paid scant regard to the north side of Russell Square, where the surviving fragment of Georgian terrace was left propped with ugly concrete buttresses. Perhaps the architect assumed that the rest of Russell Square would be

Looking north from the top floor of the UCL Engineering building, 1974. (Roger Forshaw)

demolished in due course, or he simply didn't care. It certainly seemed to lack the finesse and elegance of Lasdun's Royal College of Physicians in Regent's Park.

The inside was better, however. When it still had springy carpets and the smell of new upholstery, I played in the spacious basement auditorium with the Chelsea Opera Group. While the acoustics of the new Logan Hall weren't flattering, at least they were clear for performer and audience alike. The public foyers and stairs also had a certain grandeur.

Raw or shuttered concrete as an external finish was much favoured by many architects in the '70s, not only by Lasdun. The Camden Town Hall extension on Euston Road, completed in 1978, and Richard Seifert's 1976 building on Gray's Inn Road for the newly-merged *Times* and *Sunday Times* newspapers were from the same stable, crudely sculpted concrete which quickly attracted the dirt of passing traffic. My Hampstead girlfriend was working next door in an office in Elm Street at the time, so I saw this with my own eyes. At least Seifert must have been relieved that New Printing House Square, as it was known, had an immediate tenant. His earlier office tower at Centre Point had lain empty for ten years before its first occupant arrived in 1975.

Bloomsbury's hospital architects were up to the same tricks. Llewelyn-Davies and Weeks' ten-storey pile for the Institute of Neurology between Queen Square and Guildford Street, completed in 1978, is just about as unattractive a use of concrete as you can get.

To be fair, Patrick Hodgkinson apparently always envisaged that the external finish of the concrete at the Brunswick Centre should be painted, but this didn't happen at the time. Unfortunate residents and shoppers had to endure thirty years of increasing shabbiness until the recent excellent refurbishment.

Bloomsbury was at least spared one piece of megalomania. Mooted by Abercrombie in 1943, but carried forward by Leslie Martin and Colin St John Wilson through the 1960s, was the plan to expand the British Museum and to demolish all the properties south of Great Russell Street as far as New Oxford Street, creating a long vista to Smirke's monumental Grecian portico. Only Hawksmoor's smoke-blackened St George's would have survived. In 1973 Camden Council published *Bloomsbury: the Case against Destruction*, jointly signed by Frank Dobson,

Museum Tavern, 1973. (Nova Munda Photographic)

then leader of the Council, Alderman Martin Morton, leader of the opposition, and Lena Jeger, who was the current MP for Holborn and St Pancras. The Council recommended vacant railway land at King's Cross as an alternative.

The scheme was mercifully finally abandoned in 1974 when the government decided to acquire a new site immediately west of St Pancras Station to build a new British Library. Some tried to call this new location Bloomsbury, but that was stretching it a bit. Colin St John Wilson was given the architectural commission and set to work in his Hackney and then Islington offices. Even though this vast project didn't actually start on site until 1982 and wasn't opened by the Queen until 1998, it is one of the most remarkable buildings to have been designed, if not built, in the 1970s.

Some of Bloomsbury's oldest houses were at risk simply through scandalous neglect, rather than any proposals for demolition. Several very early eighteenth-century houses in Great Ormond Street were rescued from the clutches of the Rugby Estate by Camden Council in 1975.

Despite all this, 1970s' Bloomsbury held many charms. I had been taken a couple of times by my previous Cambridge girlfriend, when she was studying violin at the Guildhall, to the Conway Hall in Red Lion Square. Here, despite the dingy lighting and uncomfortable seating, I'd been entranced by the magic of the Allegri Quartet. More mundanely, Bloomsbury's concentration of university buildings and teaching hospitals felt familiar to me after Cambridge. The streets thronged with students, rather than the tourists of today. One wonders indeed who actually stayed in all those grotty hotels in the 1970s.

While Bloomsbury perhaps lacked the gastronomic variety of Fitzrovia, there were some excellent cheap cafés, more often as not run by Italians, such as the Cosmoba in Cosmo Place and Mille Pini in Boswell Street. The Salvation Army and YWCA canteens offered institutional

Demolishing and rebuilding the east end of Great Ormond Street, 1974. (English Heritage)

lunches, and 75p would buy roast turkey and semolina pudding. More exotically, the Ganpath and Goan in Gray's Inn Road were excellent spicy stomach-fillers.

Although many of Bloomsbury's fine selection of pubs survive and prosper to the present day, not much changed, two hostelries which I discovered in the 1970s sadly do not. The Sun at the junction of Great Ormond Street and Lamb's Conduit Street was justly famous as a free-house serving an extraordinary range of strong cask beers which the enthusiastic landlord stocked in the capacious cellars under the road. In those days it was a more popular rendezvous than the nearby Lamb. The other, which I went to only once, was its diminutive sister, the Moon, tucked away on the corner of New North Street and Boswell Court, a tiny local, and one of London's smallest pubs. With so much academia and so many institutional establishments, it never really occurred to me that there could be many permanent residents in Bloomsbury. I probably assumed it was like the centre of Cambridge. I didn't think for a moment, nice though it might be, that I would one day end up living there.

✎ COVENT GARDEN ✎

Covent Garden, or at least parts of it, was already familiar territory when I came to London and started to piece together bits of the jigsaw that seemed to comprise such a sprawling city. Several times as a teenager I had attended auditions in the Friends Meeting House, St Martin's Lane, for the National Youth Orchestra. I had also been taken to the Royal Opera House by my Chalk Farm uncle who, as an opera fanatic, saw pretty much every production. In the 1960s there were no restrictions in the side streets where he would park his beaten-up Mini Traveller, and I was used to squelching through the cabbage leaves, squashed tomatoes and banana skins of the vegetable market after the show. I also knew some of the smoke-filled dive bars where he met his thespian friends.

Now on my own two feet, I bought cheap tickets, usually in the Upper Slips, to see *Don Carlos*, *Billy Budd*, *The Rake's Progress*, *Wozzeck* and *Ice Break*, with conductors such as Georg Solti, Edward Downes and Colin Davies directing the stars of the day, including Geraint Evans, Heather Harper, Peter Glossop, Richard Van Allan, Michael Langdon, Marie Collier and Tom Allen. I also started going regularly to the Coliseum, where Sadler's Wells Opera had relocated from Rosebery Avenue in 1968 and where in 1974 they were renamed the English National Opera. Charles Mackerras, Reginald Goodall and Alexander Gibson ruled the rostrum, with Rita Hunter as Brunhilde and Willard White as Leporello in *Don Giovanni*.

Outside in the streets, away from the magnificence of Frank Matcham's theatre, I became aware that the mother of all conservation battles had been going on, probably the most seminal campaign to save an area, rather than an individual building, ever to take place in London.

I was disappointed that the market was moving out, but as a provincial teenager I hadn't known that Covent Garden Flower, Fruit and Vegetable Market had been taken out of the ownership of the Bedford Estate and nationalised in 1962, and was unaware of the 1968 Act of Parliament which authorised its closure and removal to another less crowded site. Perhaps it was the opera-going politicians sitting in the more expensive seats who had decided that such mundane and sordid activities were unsuitable in a prestigious district of central London. It was certainly an attitude I was to encounter before long at Smithfield.

Nobody indeed seemed much concerned about the loss and relocation of the market, but what provoked the storm of protest were the proposals for comprehensive redevelopment of not just some of the historic market buildings, but over 60 per cent of the surrounding area. The Covent Garden Community Association (CGCA) had been formed in 1971 to fight these proposals, primarily to protect existing residents and small businesses who would have been evicted by the GLC's plans for new offices and hotels. One of the CGCA's most voluble activists was an architect, Jim Monahan, who was passionate about keeping central London as a place where people on low incomes could continue to live in a civilised environment. All that was under threat as big business threatened to rip the heart out of the area. The scheme even included widening the Strand on its north side to create a six-lane motorway, partly in a tunnel.

Many others joined the fight. Simon Jenkins campaigned effectively in the *Evening Standard*, while the Civic Trust added its voice to the outcry.

The Tory government was put in an awkward position, not wishing to undermine Sir Desmond Plummer and the Conservative-run GLC. They therefore outwardly backed the GLC scheme but while doing so, in January 1973, Geoffrey Rippon as Secretary of State for the Environment, supported by the Home Secretary Robert Carr, listed 250 buildings. Comprehensive redevelopment was no longer possible. Later in 1973, Labour took control of the GLC and threw out the Tory plans. Eight of the nine sites earmarked for demolition were changed to refurbishment.

The old Vegetable Market closed in 1974, with little fuss or ceremony, mainly because there had been a gradual transfer of operations to the spacious new site at Nine Elms, sixty-four acres of redundant railway yards between Vauxhall and Battersea. A sign of the times was that despite the previous use of the land, no link was made to the adjacent railway lines and the only access to New Covent Garden was by road.

Covent Garden
Market, from
James Street, 1971.
(English Heritage)

One journalist ran the headline, 'Where will all the rats go when they close Covent Garden Market, after 300 years'. It was alleged that thousands of rodents, robbed of their rotten apples and sacks of potatoes, would invade local homes. Bert Jacobs, one of the market porters, was reported to have said that some of the rats were 'as big as cats'. Even the *Washington Tri-City Herald* in America ran the story, thinking perhaps that their readership might be concerned about the well-being of Eliza Doolittle from *My Fair Lady*. As it happened, no Pied Piper was needed and the rats retreated happily into the sewers.

While Covent Garden roused great passion in some, the great-and-the-good at the Opera House were probably more interested at the time in a special exhibition at the Victoria and Albert Museum. 'The Destruction of the Country House', put on by Roy Strong, Marcus Binney, Fiona Reynolds and George Monbiot in 1974 raised public awareness of another conservation issue, and was followed in 1975 by the founding of SAVE Britain's Heritage.

The refurbishment of Covent Garden didn't happen overnight. The GLC started work in 1977 on repairing and converting Fowler's 1830s market buildings in the centre of the piazza for small shops and a space for a covered flea market. The London Transport Museum began the restoration of Cubitt's 1871 Flower Market in the south-east corner of the piazza in 1978. Both were open for business in 1980. However, the Jubilee Hall, still scheduled for demolition, lay empty, and had to be 'saved' by a later campaign. Nobody knew what to do with E.M. Barry's magnificent 1859 Floral Hall, until Jeremy Dixon's inspired boldness in the 1990s.

Piecemeal repair and infill in the surrounding streets began slowly, and seven of the empty sites were colonised by local residents as community gardens, of which only Phoenix Gardens behind Charing Cross Road survives today. Fred Collins tended the plot in Earlham Street as well as running the local ironmongers, founded by his grandfather.

Some of the 1970s infill was not as good as it might have been. The GLC's housing scheme in Odhams Walk, begun in 1974, connected poorly with the street, and was too inward-looking. Richard Seifert's offices on the north side of Long Acre, albeit reduced in size, were unfortunately sunk into a basement well, thus preventing any ground-floor shops, particularly stupid with hindsight. It is a sobering thought that much of Covent Garden might

Work in progress in 1978 on the main market hall, Covent Garden. (English Heritage)

have looked like this had the whole-scale redevelopment plans proceeded. The hideous hotel (now a Travelodge) and offices at the top of Drury Lane, astride High Holborn, both built in 1972, slipped through the net before the madness was abandoned. At least the Winter Gardens, further south on Drury Lane, incorporated a new theatre, rather tamely called the New London Theatre and home for over twenty years to Andrew Lloyd Webber's *Cats*, but the flats and car park piled above do little to enhance any sense of enclosure to the street.

For a while, in the hiatus after the conservation battle, Covent Garden enjoyed the frisson of being highly 'alternative'; in today's parlance, it was a 'cool' place to hang out. Although the cockney market porters might have migrated south, the pub landlords and their brusque manners certainly had not. Taverns such as the Nags Head in James Street, the Essex Serpent in King Street and even the Lamb and Flag in Rose Street retained an earthy roughness. For those seeking more gentility there were always the theatre pubs, such as the Marquis of Anglesea in Bow Street opposite the Royal Opera House, or the Lemon Tree and the Welsh Harp, the latter effectively a stage door for the Coliseum.

Amid the uncertainty there were pioneers who seized the moment. We eagerly attended the Campaign for Real Ale's first ever beer festival in September 1975, held in one of the empty market buildings. It was such a success that in 1977 they decided to do something on a grander scale, but this time at Alexandra Palace where there was more space. In 1976 Nicholas Saunders took a lease on a derelict warehouse between Short's Gardens and Monmouth Street and set up a whole food shop, where grains, pulses and dried fruits were sold unpackaged with no frills. Neal's Yard rapidly became a trendy destination, soon expanding into a bakery, dairy and greengrocer, and an empire was born. At No. 27 Monmouth Street, the Monmouth Coffee Co. began roasting beans in the basement and opened a sampling café upstairs, as well as selling green beans to roast at home. The smell wafted into the street and it was a pleasure and temptation just to pass by. Their commercial success compelled the adjoining owners to commission Levitt Bernstein Architects to refurbish the rest of this street block in 1978. Similarly derelict seventeenth and eighteenth-century houses between Mercers Street and Shelton Street in the so-called Comyn Ching triangle (named after a long-established ironmonger's shop) were imaginatively rescued and restored by Terry Farrell, starting in 1977, and now known as Ching Court.

Not everything, of course, was new or under threat. Many businesses that had been there for years simply carried on regardless. Rules restaurant in Maiden Lane was a bastion of tradition, Moss Bros was where you hired top hats and morning coats, Stamford's in Long Acre was the best map shop in the world and, a few doors along, Paxman's made and sold their own French horns. Mr Sullivan even carried on the Ellen Keeley family business of making and repairing traditional wooden market barrows in his Neal Street workshop, until the developers forced his hand.

Some people today disparage Covent Garden, saying that it has sold out to tourism and the commercialisation of souvenir shops and fast food. The journalist Tom Dyckhoff has recently described the 1970s campaign as a Pyrrhic victory. Higher rents have indeed taken their toll,

Mr Sullivan at work in Neal Street.
(Theo Bergstrom)

on Paxman's for one. However, what the critics overlook is that many of the 'tourists' are in fact Londoners who like going there, and the chain stores are part of the globalisation that afflicts every shopping street in the country. The saving of Covent Garden was, and still is, a remarkable feat, and proved a successful and inspirational model for many other community groups to follow.

∽ KENSINGTON ∽

Readers so far may have noticed a distinctly North London focus, gradually moving towards the centre. As someone who had grown up in Cambridge, sixty miles north of London, it was probably natural to have homed in on those bits I already knew. It is sometimes said that migrants to London congregate and settle near where they first arrived in the capital, hence the Irish in Camden Town near Euston or the Indian community in Southall close to Heathrow, even Aussies in Earl's Court near the West London coach terminal. The theory even accounts for West Indians in Brixton. The first wave of immigrants who came off the HMS *Windrush* in 1948 were housed in the deep shelter at Clapham South and registered for work at the Lambeth Labour Exchange on Coldharbour Lane. Maybe someone has done a dissertation to explain all this. I suspect that chance (good luck or bad), convenience and the size of one's pocket all play a big part in where one ends up.

So it was in September 1974 when Brynly arrived in London. I had first known him as a larger-than-life lad from Somerset playing in the National Youth Orchestra and now, two years after me, he had finished his degree at Cambridge and come to London to try his luck as a freelance bassoonist, being seen as something of a 'star' young player. Bryn was looking for somewhere to live, and knew of my current plight of having no fixed abode, camping on other people's floors and using my car as a glorified suitcase. A tip-off from two girls at the Royal College of Music had directed Bryn to a vacant flat in the house where they were living, just around the corner from the college in Prince Consort Road.

Queen's Gate Terrace was one of the grander streets running east to west between Queen's Gate and Gloucester Road, lined with tall mid-Victorian terraces faced in stucco. The road was so wide that cars parked in the middle as well as kerbside. The scale of the buildings was like those in Belgravia, and as big as the terraced house ever became in London. No. 54 was on the north side, the last white stucco before the grey brick corner with Gloucester Road.

The premises on offer were the first-floor flat. The whole house was owned by a property company who had done little in the way of repairs or maintenance to this particular building for years. We got the key from their agents, and after the most cursory of visits decided to take it. Even though the flat hadn't been lived in for a while and had an unpleasant mustiness, the address alone, after the suburbs of Hendon, seemed too good to be true.

The house must originally have been intended for a very large, well-to-do family and a host of servants, with a mews at the back for the horses, carriage and ostlers. Sometime, perhaps quite early on in the twentieth century, it had been converted into flats, with at least one per floor.

Mrs Good lived in the front half of the basement, a docile and long-suffering old lady who had been there for years and had few good words for the landlord. Mrs Howell had the rooms at the back part of the basement, a rather brusque lady who had few words for anyone. On the ground floor were violinist Kathy and trumpeter/pianist Helen, our contacts from the college. Above us, on the second floor, was Mr Watt, a taciturn gentleman somehow involved in the legal profession, who with his shabby suit and slightly wild eyes looked more like a scarecrow. The third floor was supposedly occupied (according to the electoral register) but there was no sign of anyone actually being there. The fourth and top floor of this six-storey mansion was definitely vacant when we moved in, the door firmly locked.

The entrance portico and front entrance steps were palatial, even though the paint and plaster were peeling off the columns. Inside the massive front door the tiled entrance hall was almost uncomfortably generous, leading to a wide and gently rising staircase with ornate cast-iron balusters and a mahogany handrail. Off the first floor landing, double doors opened into our flat.

The first floor or 'piano nobile' would originally have been the principal drawing room for the house, a full-width front room perhaps connected by tall folding doors to a single deep rear room, enabling maximum flexibility for entertaining. Our flat, comprising over 1,200 sq. ft, had been carved out of this space to create five rooms, a spacious hall big enough for a dining table, plus a bathroom and a kitchen. One added benefit of being end-of-terrace was that our flat extended beyond and behind the stairs, housing the long thin kitchen and a third front bedroom.

Five rooms meant five people. Bryn, Robin, Tim and I made up a Cambridge quartet, the first three all from Corpus Christi. A fourth 'corpuscle' dropped out so I asked a Canadian horn player

View from the balcony of the flat, No. 54 Queen's Gate Terrace, 1974. (Author's Collection)

whom I'd recently met playing in a band and who was studying with Ifor James and Alan Civil at the Royal College Music. Geoff couldn't believe his luck. We moved in on 5 October 1974.

Bryn took the best room at the front, south facing and with three full-height French windows with curved fanlights opening onto the balcony, which ran the entire width of the house, including a deeper section over the portico. Because of its size, and the gas fire built into the opening of the pompous black marble fireplace, this bedroom also became our sitting room. Conveniently Bryn was extremely sociable and habitually the last to go to bed (and last to rise in the morning).

The bathroom with loo, sink and bath was separated from Geoff's room by a long narrow corridor, still with a 15ft-high ceiling (good for climbing practice) which led to my room at the back. This annex was built on stilts, a cubic pod stuck onto the back of the building and effectively exposed to the elements on five of its six sides. In winter it was an ice box. When I was away one cold January weekend, a cord snapped on the large heavy sash in my room. On my return a snowdrift had accumulated on my bed, blown in through the gaping window.

The flat came with some rudimentary furniture, a bed in each room, several rickety wardrobes and threadbare carpets. The prize item was a black Naugahyde sofa in the main room, surprisingly comfortable but sticky in hot weather. Today it could be an exhibit in the modern section of the Geffrye Museum.

Apart from Bryn's gas fire and the dodgy gas stove in the kitchen, we relied on antiquated electric heaters. The unventilated bathroom had an archaic Ascot gas geyser whose fumes added to the fug when running, or more accurately, dribbling, a bath. This tiny room was a constraining feature of the flat, and it helped that we didn't all get up at the same time in the morning. A poem was stuck on the inside of the door:

If I'm in bed please refrain
From having bath or pulling chain,
Do not sing and do not shout,
Keep it quiet and clear off out.

Having dutifully paid the rent, which the agents had asked for when we first moved in, we applied to the Council to set a fair rent. Robin's father happened to know the Rent Officer for Kensington and Chelsea, and we duly made sure that the flat did not look overly glamorous on the day of the inspection. The rent for the whole flat was reduced to £120 per month, not bad divided between five of us. We were also tipped off that the cost of any improvements such as redecoration could be taken off the rent. We had a party to celebrate, the first of many.

The agents didn't seem to mind, but perhaps the property company did, because within a few months we were informed that there was a new owner, a Mr Abidi. His intention, we were told, was to reclaim the whole house for his extended family to live in. We, thankfully, had full tenants' rights, a legal agreement signed with the agents, and a fair rent, so we weren't going to be a pushover. Poor Mrs Good was given a harder time and eventually, after lots of pressure, she was bought out ridiculously cheaply. Abidi's agents even chopped down the fine fig tree which grew in the front basement light-well.

Because of Geoff, the flat became something of a Mecca for Canadians, mainly from Vancouver or Toronto. Flute-playing Chris arrived from British Columbia and shared Geoff's room, building a bed-deck and converting the wardrobe into an indoor garden centre to grow 'exotic' plants. Disappointingly, even with arc lights and excellent compost filched from the death-throes of the Chelsea Flower Show, the output was poor. The legal tomatoes on the balcony did better. I bought a piano from an advert in the *Evening News* (still in the 1970s a rival to and unmerged with the *Evening Standard*), a modern Boyd upright in excellent condition, and a bargain at £20. We hired a van to rescue some furniture from the empty house in Hendon and pick up the piano. At least in my isolated bedroom my practice disturbed no one.

Generally, the sound-proofing was good, with thick party walls and floors. We never heard Helen's trumpet downstairs, and Mr Watt upstairs was uncomplaining, even after the wildest of our frequent parties. What is more surprising is that the front balcony didn't collapse under the weight of revellers.

I hadn't really known much about Kensington before moving there, apart from the Albert Hall and the Royal College of Music. I'd been to several Promenade concerts, memorably seeing Pierre Boulez conduct and Jessye Norman sing in Schoenberg's *Gurrelieder* in August 1973. I'd stayed overnight in Jonny Ash's basement flat in Cornwall Gardens, before he'd moved to Finchley Road.

Although Kensington had the reputation for being the fanciest part of town, it was by no means consistently smart in the 1970s. Our house was not the only one with shabby stucco and crumbling cornices and there were plenty of multi-occupied properties like ours.

The local shops were generally expensive. The small Waitrose on the opposite corner with Gloucester Road was nicknamed the rip-off store, and used as a last resort. The Aerated Bread Co., whose bread was baked in Camden Town, was reasonable and didn't hike its prices because of its location. We never used the nearby Fleur-de-Lys patisserie. Our local parade was a curious mix: Palace Gate Pet Stores, the Whirlpool Launderette, the Gondoliere restaurant and, before long, a Pizza Express.

Kensington High Street was more like Oxford Street, and the big attraction here for the world at large, if not the young men of No. 54 Queen's Gate Terrace, was the Big BIBA. BIBA's had moved into Derry and Tom's old department store in 1973, having started out in smaller premises nearby. Now sprawling over seven floors, BIBA's was eulogised as 'the sexiest shop on earth', 'a heavenly mix of Rock-and-Roll decadence and Art Nouveau chic'. Behind its

The ground floor of BIBA's department store, Kensington High Street, 1975. (English Heritage)

blacked-out windows it maintained a unique atmosphere, with different themes on each floor, all unified by the Art Deco BIBA logo. On the fifth floor was the Rainbow restaurant, and at the very top the spectacular one-and-a-half acre Kensington Roof Garden.

At its zenith the 'Dream Emporium' drew a multitude of customers each week, but by 1975 its finances were out of control and its owners and instigators, Barbara Hulanicki and Stephen Fitz-Simon, sold out to Dorothy Perkins, who promptly closed it down. I went there several times but it never seemed a sensible place to buy baked beans, although plenty of people did for the Andy Warhol packaging. I suspect that many people went just to look or be seen, rather than to spend serious money. The really wealthy continued to shop at Harrods or Fortnum and Mason's.

The BIBA fantasy was dead and even when a replica was re-launched under different management in Mayfair in 1978, it folded within two years. In Kensington High Street there was still Barkers department store, very dull compared to BIBA's, and I never had any inclination or necessity to go in there.

Life in the faded grandeur of Queen's Gate Terrace was everything one might have expected and more, where the predictable masculine arguments over kitties, rotas, time spent in the bath, the mountains of washing up and the containment of grease in the kitchen were offset by a strong communal spirit, and a constant stream of visitors, male and female, probably quite

The Builders' Arms, Kensington Court Place, 1975. (English Heritage)

daunting for the latter. I never really found out whether there was a strong local community out there on the streets, although the impression was one of transience, of people passing through. We were our own community, made our own fun, and found the best places to drink.

The nearest pubs were unpromising. The Gloucester, on the corner with Victoria Grove, was a dump, and the Harrington, just beyond Waitrose, little better, although there was a snooker hall upstairs and they did serve Courage Director's beer. Our quest was good, well-kept real ale, a cause readily adopted by the Canadian contingent, and our favourite local quickly became the Builders' Arms, a five-minute walk from the flat along St Alban's Grove, at the corner with Kensington Court Place. This was a Charrington's tied house, with crimson flock wallpaper, a stained but patterned carpet and comfortable, if worn, red velvet upholstery. It was rarely crowded and there were benches and tables outside at the front for sunny weather. Best of all, the IPA draught beer was excellent, at 24p per pint, or four pints for under £1. On the opposite corner was a Thai restaurant where the sign-writer had made the 'i' look like a 't'. When it changed its name to Siam Cuisine, the 'i' ended up looking like an 'l'.

When feeling more energetic we went further afield. Twenty minutes on foot took us to the Anglesea Arms in Selwood Terrace with its selection of strong ales, Ruddle's County, Wadworth's 6X and Theakston's Old Peculier. For cockney character we went to the Warwick Arms and Britannia Tap in Warwick Road, two pubs almost side by side, with wonderfully ornate landladies serving Fullers and Young's. The Churchill in Kensington Church Street was also worth the walk. On bikes we ventured further, the Star in Belgrave Mews West behind the German embassy always a good bet for the full range of Fullers' beers.

We generally ignored the nearest 'famous' pub to the flat, the Queens Arms in Queen's Gate Terrace Mews. Long known as the Ninety-Nine, because the nearby Royal College of Music had ninety-eight rooms, it was overcrowded with students or audience from the Albert Hall, and only sold keg beer. If we wanted a student haunt we bluffed our way into the JCR bar of Imperial College. This was on an upper floor of one of their 1960s buildings (by Sheppard Robson and now demolished) on the south side of Princes Gardens, and had

Kensington Gardens, 1975. (Geoffrey Pearce)

the merit, so it seemed at the time, of selling Newcastle Brown Ale in bottles. Pubs generally didn't have televisions and we went there to watch Joe Bugner fight Muhammad Ali, live from Kuala Lumpur.

Kensington Gardens and Hyde Park were on our doorstep. While they might have lacked the hills and woods of Hampstead Heath, they were nevertheless a huge playground and were beautifully kept by the Royal Parks Agency. I don't know if we realised how lucky we were to live so close to such an oasis. We probably simply took it for granted.

Frisbee and football were our usual pastimes, and in the swelteringly hot summers of 1976 and 1977 we swam in the Serpentine when on stiflingly hot evenings it was bliss to plunge into the warm brown water. It was actually cleaner than it looked, as the Serpentine by now was fed from the mains rather than the Westbourne sewer, and was mildly chlorinated. The south side was roped off from the rowing boats to provide a lido. On the banks and in the deckchairs, reptilian sun-worshippers soaked up the rays from April to October, turning into leathery wrinkled lizards. One or two hardy freaks apparently swam every day of the year.

Speakers' Corner in the 1970s still attracted animated crowds and while orange-box oratory was no doubt in decline, not everyone was a crank or comedian. Donald Soper was still a regular on his soap-box.

Hyde Park was unfenced and open at all times, but not so Kensington Gardens; some would even shudder to hear it called a public park. It certainly had a more refined air. On warm spring and autumn afternoons nannies pushed their precious cargoes in prams past the herbaceous borders and elderly dowagers gingerly took the air, accompanied by their prim housekeepers, before retiring somewhere smart for tea. On a few occasions, egged on by alcohol-fuelled group bravura, we climbed over the railings after dark and roamed around the Gardens; fortunately we were never caught by the roving patrols, whose headlights could be seen from afar.

At the beginning of the Cold War, the avenue of elms along the Broad Walk had been felled under the pretext of public safety, but more likely for civil defence purposes (where better in central London to land a light aircraft and evacuate the Queen?). In the early 1970s the tree sprites took their revenge when Dutch Elm Disease ravaged both Hyde Park and Kensington Gardens and saw the culling of 500 trees, replanted with spindly saplings which seemed scant replacement at the time. Now too the park wardens were doing their utmost to stop skateboarders (the latest craze) from using this runway, with its alluring slope towards Kensington Gore. At least no one had yet invented rollerblades.

In terms of building development, Kensington appeared less active and less threatened in the mid-1970s than the other parts of central London which I knew about. Richard Seifert had already stamped his mark with two hotels, the horrible slab of the Royal Garden right on the edge of Kensington Gardens, and the fifteen-storey Grand Metropolitan at Albert Gate, completed in 1973. Some people were still muttering about Basil Spence's Knightsbridge Barracks, finished in 1970, whose 100m tower was a severe intrusion into the Arcadian idyll of the park. Spence had also designed the new Kensington and Chelsea Town Hall, which was being built in Hornton Street and finished in 1977, a massive pile of red bricks supposedly blending with the existing library next door. I never saw the fine 1830s villas that were pulled down in 1972 to create the site. Nor was I around ten years later when the Council decided overnight, instructed by their leader Nicholas Freeman, to demolish the old Town Hall on the High Street, pre-empting any possible risk of a preservation order.

Of the original five, Tim was the first to leave the flat, heading off to share a maisonette with his sister in St John's Wood. He had been working for Stiles Breen, one of the local solicitors in Harrow, and was possibly slightly concerned that his legal career might be jeopardised if the flat ever got busted by the police. You never knew what they might find in the wardrobe.

Besides, Bryn by this time had become increasingly involved with the Workers' Revolutionary Party and its Trotskyite ideals, and was rumoured to have visited the 'Red House' in Derbyshire, a training centre owned by Corin and Vanessa Redgrave. Mao Tse-tung (still in his dotage), Brezhnev and Salvador Allende were frequent subjects for argument in the flat, together with the merits or otherwise of Baader-Meinhof, Black September and the Red Brigade.

Bryn was even selling their newspaper *Newsline* on the street, and one of his comrade vendors, Nigel, was irritating the hell out of rest of us by ringing the door bell at six o'clock each morning to get Bryn out of bed. It was a fruitless task, waking everyone except Bryn. Geoff eventually chased him down the street with a broom handle, stark naked. Nigel never returned.

Geoff was the next to leave, for an orchestral job and a new life in Belgium, leaving Chris to carry on repairing flutes and mending bikes, and instigating a fresh influx of Canadians. One of these, the vivacious Gale, managed to find a way into the top floor and squatted there with her jovial boyfriend, Colin, a dead-ringer for a baby-faced Frank Bruno.

Without Tim and Geoff the community spirit wasn't quite the same. By the spring of 1977 I too was looking to move out. The big wide property market beckoned.

∽ GETTING AROUND TOWN ∽

Having been virtually born and bred on two wheels in Cambridge, my trusty bike came with me to London, where I was surprised to find that the bicycle was almost an endangered species. Clearly certain parts of London were challengingly hilly (although much of the centre is reasonably flat), and the scale of the metropolis made many journeys prohibitively long, but there seemed to be no culture of cycling, even for short distances, and very few people seemed to own bikes. Most regarded it as a dangerous and mildly eccentric means of transport, perhaps with some justification in the undulating suburbs. When I cycled from Hendon to work in Harrow, my colleagues thought I was mad.

The idea of actually encouraging cycling in London appeared to be a complete anathema to anyone in officialdom in the 1970s. My brother, who doggedly pedalled from West Hampstead to his lab in Bloomsbury, campaigned with Friends of the Earth to improve facilities at Swiss Cottage, including what then seemed the revolutionary idea of installing bike racks outside the public library and swimming pool. Camden Council, of course, had no budget for such frivolities and it was left to FOE to procure them, kindly donated in the end by the manufacturers, Fischers.

Safety measures such as protective helmets, high-visibility Gore-Tex jackets and flashing halogen lights were not yet available, not even thought about, although my brother had invented an ingenious bike-light system with rechargeable batteries hidden in the main tube of the frame. Sadly, he didn't patent it.

Nor were there Kevlar tyres. Punctures were common and a repair kit was an essential piece of equipment, carried at all times. Bicycle repair shops were a rarity, hence the FOE experiment at Swiss Cottage. Angel Cycles in St John Street, Islington, was an exception, run by a delightfully cheery man in a long brown coat and with immensely thick spectacles. He took so much pleasure listening to the Third Programme's classical music wafting from the radio in the shop that he often forgot to charge his customers.

Bike and bus lanes and dedicated cycle tracks were not yet on the local authority agenda. Some authorities actively discouraged cycling, notably in the Royal Parks. My brother, among others, had been frustrated that there was no direct north-south route across Regent's Park. The same applied in Hyde Park, although there was a perfect diagonal tarmac footpath from north of the Serpentine bridge to Marble Arch. I took to using this, always taking care to give any pedestrians or dogs a wide berth. One cold, wet February morning in 1976, with no one about, I was set upon by two policemen who had been hiding behind a tree, and dragged off to the little-used police station in the middle of the park to be charged with a breach in the regulations. Incensed by such idiocy, I attended when summonsed by the Marylebone Magistrates' Court. I correctly pleaded guilt to the offence and was fined 50p, probably the minimum possible, and with no costs. The bench suggested that the policemen might have better ways of spending their time.

The London Cycling Campaign was launched in September 1978. As a publicity stunt they organised a quartet of races between bike, car and public transport from Shoreditch, Brixton, Kentish Town and Notting Hill to the Embankment. The bike won every time, which proved a point about speed if not safety. Their first piece of direct action in December 1978 was to implement, using white tape and cardboard signs, a scheme at Albert Gate, Knightsbridge, which had been turned down by the GLC.

In the Kensington flat, Geoff and Chris became enthusiastic cyclists. The landlord disapproved of bikes in the common parts so we parked them in our rooms. Not everyone was so keen. One trip into the Chilterns and a tumble through a hedge on a steep bend put Tim off the idea, although he and Bryn acquired motorbikes. Cycling, motorised or otherwise, had its dangers. Potholes, spilt oil and ice, bolshy taxi drivers and their unannounced U-turns, opening doors of parked cars and oblivious pedestrians were hazards which required assertive alertness.

For me, despite the risks, the bicycle became the most illuminating way of getting to know London: free, fast, independent, easy to park and, with a pair of panniers, the best way to carry bulky shopping and a bassoon. Those unfortunates who travelled everywhere by tube in their subterranean world never had a chance of putting together all the component parts which make up London. On my bike I got to understand the strange one-way system in Camden Town and to unravel the complexities south of the river, where every road seemed to converge on the Elephant and Castle. It helped to realise that the river didn't flow in a straight west-to-east line through London, nor the bridges all cross north-south. The grid-iron plan of the West End certainly didn't apply here.

Public transport in 1970s London was either wonderful or a sore point and a constant source of jokes, depending on your point of view. The old RT buses were being phased out (the last withdrawn from service in 1979) and replaced with the Routemaster. These elegant double-deckers operated on every route, always in their red livery, except in 1977 when, as part of the Queen's Jubilee, some were painted silver. Mini-buses, midi-buses and single-decker bendy buses had not yet arrived on London's streets, or in the suburbs where the network was still strongly radial. The Green Line services had been taken over in 1970 by the National Bus Co., who gradually withdrew them from London, closing the last cross-London route in 1979. Understanding the logic and detail of London's bus numbers was an art form in itself, and my knowledge far from comprehensive. Some of the routes took seemingly epic journeys across the capital, such as the No. 2 and 2A from Norwood, which I sometimes caught to Apex Corner before hitch-hiking north, once even sharing the top deck with Sir Adrian Boult before he alighted near John Barnes.

The completion of the Victoria Line in 1972, when the final station at Pimlico opened, had been a boost for London, the first new Underground line for half a century. The extension of the Piccadilly Line to Heathrow opened in December 1977. There was even brave talk of two new projects, the Chelsea-Hackney Line and the Fleet Line (later to become the Jubilee Line, the first part of which opened in 1979). The French, however, seemed to be light years ahead when in December 1977 President Giscard D'Estaing opened the new RER, a regional express train running right under and across Paris. In London, we were going backwards with the closure of the Snow Hill tunnel in 1970 and the reduction of services to Broad Street, still living in the shadow of Dr Beeching. Thameslink and Crossrail were decades away, not even on the drawing board in the 1970s. By the mid-1970s, Broad Street Station was dilapidated, with trees growing between the disused platforms and the French Renaissance façade neglected and crumbling.

There were worries that British Rail might close the North London Line altogether, because they claimed it was so little used. Friends of the Earth in Camden had been campaigning to have the line shown on the Underground map so that more people knew about it, but the authorities refused. Many others took up the cause, and in a brilliant piece of direct action people went around with black marker-pens and drew in the line on the maps wherever they were displayed in stations or public places. After a successful example of consumer pressure the 'crazy railway' was saved, and with it the best way to reach Kew Gardens from North London, taking you through places such as Willesden Junction, which you'd never dreamt existed. Even when Broad Street Station was eventually closed and redeveloped for Broadgate, the NLL survived.

The railways were still nationalised, as they had been since the war, and British Rail appeared painfully slow to invest in improvements. Much of their rolling stock was antiquated, particularly the slam-door carriages with isolated compartments on Southern Region. High-speed trains, christened the InterCity 125, were eventually introduced in 1977 from Paddington and King's Cross.

There were also concerns about safety, particularly after the ghastly Moorgate disaster in February 1975, when forty-three people were killed as the train hurtled through the buffers and ploughed into the end wall. I already had a strong aversion to the tube, which I found hot, crowded and expensive.

Apart from a small number of sightseeing boats for tourists, the Thames was unused for passenger traffic. As with the demise of the Clyde steamers and ferries in Scotland throughout the 1970s, no one gave any thought to the potential of London's river for public transport.

The overwhelming preoccupation for London in the 1970s was what to do with the roads. This, of course, wasn't a fresh issue. The idea of building new urban motorways in London had their origins in the 1937 Highway Development Survey and in the 1943 Abercrombie Plan, which envisaged a 'brave new world' after the war. During the '60s, however, more precise plans for a series of concentric Ringways were developed by the GLC and published in 1967.

The post-war boom in car ownership (12 million in Britain by 1970) and the love affair with the automobile showed no sign of abating. At Milton Keynes, a new city was being built with grid-iron boulevards and central car parks to cater entirely for the private car, as if modelled on the sprawling low-rise of Los Angeles. Now was crunch time for London.

The Hammersmith and Chiswick flyover, built in the 1960s, already showed what was potentially in store. The Westway public inquiry failed to stop the completion of two and a half miles of elevated motorway in 1970, but it raised sufficient issues to allow many of the major policies to be queried. In 1971 Peter Walker, then Secretary of State for the Environment, set up the Urban Motorways Committee in the face of a rising tide of hostile public opinion. The findings were that the urban motorways already built and those projected resulted in unacceptable visual intrusion, severance of communities and noise, and that far more money would have to be spent than had previously been anticipated. More powers would need to be given to local authorities to acquire and treat land outside the highway limit. There wasn't much questioning of the need for the motorways in the first place, more about the cost.

That, however, was enough to instil scepticism in the Treasury and Department of Transport, although the GLC blundered on with their plans and began construction of some of the early parts of the Ringway scheme, notably the motorway spur from Westway down to Shepherd's Bush and the East Cross route either side of the Blackwall Tunnel. It seemed only a matter of

Broad Street Station, 1976. (English Heritage)

Archway Road in 1970, before widening. (English Heritage)

time before the North Cross route would be driven through Chalk Farm, Camden, Islington and Hackney, closely following the route of the North London railway line. The Layfield Report on the public inquiry into the GLC's Greater London Development Plan dealt with 28,000 objections, mostly to do with the road proposal. Layfield's bombshell, when published in February 1973, was to conclude that Ringway One, including the North, East and West Cross routes, should be built. So much for listening! Such madness, of course, was not confined to London. As Alan Bennett noted sardonically, the 'Welcome to Leeds' sign on the M1 used to say 'Motorway City of the Seventies'.

The Department of Transport (DoT) had their own agenda and their own schemes. In North London in 1971, they had widened the section of the Archway Road from the Archway roundabout up to and underneath the Hornsey Lane bridge, in so doing demolishing the historic Whittington almshouses which had stood near the foot of the hill. The middle section of Holloway Road at the Nag's Head junction had already been expanded into a six-lane dual carriageway in the 1960s. Their plan was to widen the whole of Holloway Road and the northern part of Archway Road through Highgate.

As part of the improvement of London's trunk roads, they built the Elephant and Castle gyratories and Old Street roundabout and planned to do the same at the Angel junction, with or without an underpass. The groundswell of articulate opposition, which arose first to challenge these monstrous proposals and eventually to see them scrapped, was a new phenomenon. Campaigners such as Tony Aldous made a name for themselves.

Even before they seized control of the GLC in the April 1973, the Labour Party had pledged to scrap Ringway One, amid popular acclaim. Indeed, their manifesto commitment was a big factor in their election victory. But it wasn't quite so straightforward. When Illtyd Harrington, as deputy to the new GLC leader Reg Goodwin, was asked by an interviewer in 1974 what he thought was the greatest achievement after a year in office, Illtyd said that it had taken that long to persuade the GLC traffic engineers to abandon their plans. The same went for their counterparts within the DoT. They were the enemy within. The DoT shelved their plans for the Angel, but further north the battle of the Archway Road continued right through the '70s, with Nina Tuckman and George Stern in the forefront. The first public inquiry in 1978 had to be abandoned because of the severe disruption from protesters.

The tide was turned back, but not without great cost. The impact on property prices and investment in those districts, or individual streets, which had been blighted by road proposals, remained for many years, and in some cases the scars have been permanent. Nor did the abandonment of motorway construction solve the traffic problem in London.

With the closure of so many lines, rail freight was in decline and lorry traffic increasing, both in numbers and size of vehicle. Lorries on their way to and from the Channel ports came through central London. It was decided therefore to press ahead with the outer orbital road, which for the most part was in the green belt beyond the built-up limits of London. The first small section of the M25 was opened in 1975, but the whole circuit wasn't completed until 1986, which is when the first lorry ban was introduced in London.

Parking meters and yellow lines had been in use since the 1960s to control on-street parking in the West End, but that didn't stop the construction of multi-storey car parks. The new underground car park in Cavendish Square caused a fuss in 1970 when the access ramps destroyed the historic plane trees at the corners. Greater care was taken in Bloomsbury Square in 1972, where a helical spiral on seven levels was dug, occupying a smaller area and saving most of the trees at the edges.

Residents' parking controls were brought in by Kensington and Chelsea in 1976. Extraordinarily, considering how things are today, there was no charge for a permit. All you had to do was park in one of the authorised bays, although by 1977 that often meant driving round the streets late at night to find a space.

The congestion and the belching exhausts of lorries and buses exacerbated the problems of pollution. Despite the latest Clean Air Act of 1968, there were still occasional smogs. The last dense fog seriously to trouble London was in November 1974. That evening I had to abandon my car near the Serpentine bridge and fumble my way home on foot. Even sticking my head out of the window, I couldn't see the end of the bonnet.

In my Morris Minor I was not, of course, exactly helping London's traffic problems. Devoted as I was to my bicycle, owning a car had its benefits, especially when it came to girlfriends and not having to worry about train timetables. What's more, the Morris had an excellent heater, unlike Robin's air-cooled Volkswagen Beetle, which was freezing in winter.

Regulations and restrictions were much laxer than they are today. The wearing of seatbelts was not compulsory, despite Jimmy Savile's TV promotion, 'Clunk Click Every Trip', launched in 1972. There was a cavalier attitude to drinking and driving, and the first breathalysers given to the police in 1967 were crude and unreliable. I had the misfortune to be stopped by the constabulary near Hammersmith bridge after a night out 'with the lads' and four pints of bitter, but got away with it by using the hyperventilating trick to dilute the alcohol on one's breath. One or two brass players were reputed to have used their strong lungs to burst the machine, and thus escape punishment.

Owning a car was not without its problems. Mine was broken into outside the Royal College of Music, stolen on Christmas Eve from Hendon and, in April 1976, crashed into at the junction of Eaton Square and Eccleston Street by an idiot doing an illegal right turn. I managed to find a panel beater whose quote was less than the write-off value. Another near-miss occurred one rainy evening when exiting the covered petrol filling station on Park Lane, slamming on my brakes to avoid a stray pedestrian. The booming voice of admonition belonged to Ian Paisley. History might have been different.

Although routine maintenance, such as adjusting the sparking plugs and tappets or changing the oil, was wonderfully easy because you could get at everything with ordinary tools, the Morris Minor had its inherent foibles. The leaking radiator and water hoses were a constant irritation.

The Electrathon, Donnington Park, 1979. (Roger Forshaw)

A slipping fan belt meant a low battery and consequent starting problems. In really cold or damp weather the crank handle wasn't much use, so it was always good to park on a downhill slope. Even then, push starting on one's own was always unnerving, running alongside with the door open, ready to jump in as soon as it gathered enough speed to put it into gear. On a hill there was the risk of leaving it too late and seeing the car run away without you. Wheel bearings were another weakness on the Morris, culminating in my rear nearside wheel coming off as I negotiated the roundabout at Shepherd's Bush. Fortunately, the car didn't fall onto its axle, and somehow I limped to a nearby garage. Opum Funf lived to fight another day and another decade. It's more than can be said for my brother's fifteen-year-old Mini, which finally bit the dust, or rust, in 1978. He managed to sell the number plate 3518 MG for £300, considerably more than the scrap value of the car.

Few people in the 1970s were overly concerned with ecological aspects of transport, apart from lorry fumes or energy efficiency. An exception was Lucas Batteries, who sponsored an open competition to find the vehicle that could travel furthest on two of their standard car batteries in two hours. My brother entered his homemade machine, a hybrid tricycle, in this first Electrathon, held at Donnington Park in 1979, and completed thirty-one miles. Beta Bikes sponsored the tricycle frame and Dowding & Mills repaired the vital lawnmower electric motor which had burnt out in trials.

Clive Sinclair had been working on a similar idea throughout the 1970s, but didn't finally produce his C5 electric car until 1985, which was met with public ridicule and commercial failure. The combustion engine ruled the world.

∞ MUNG BEANS AND CARROT CAKE ∞

While I might have promoted the benefits of the bicycle to some of my friends and colleagues, I was inducted in a big way into the complexities of organic and vegetarian food in the Kensington flat. I had been brought up on the limited diet and Mrs Beeton recipes of provincial 1950s and '60s Britain, and then fed on traditional institutional dinners in the Cambridge college dining hall, everything swimming in gravy or custard. Thereafter, in my first two years in London, I had got by on office canteen lunches and greasy spoon cafés (spending the weekly allocation of luncheon vouchers), bacon butties and baked beans, with the occasional visit to a curry or kebab house. The new world of whole food was a revelation.

In the '60s there had been a scattering of health-food shops in the smarter parts of London, selling rolled oats, white basmati rice and cornflakes made with brown sugar, but none of this was properly organic. For that you had to go to Wholefoods, the Soil Association's shop in Baker Street.

Two Californian brothers, Greg and Craig Sams, who came to London in 1967, were prominent among a clutch of pioneers who set out to revolutionise the food industry in the 1970s. Their particular interest was macrobiotics and in 1968 they had started a restaurant called Seed, operating in the rambling basement of the Gloucester Hotel in Westbourne Terrace, Paddington. John Lennon, Yoko Ono and other psychedelic celebrities took to hanging out there. In 1971 they moved into retailing and opened the Ceres Grain Store in All Saints Street, in the shadow of the Westway flyover in Notting Hill, soon expanding into two shops at the top end of Portobello Road. That is where Geoff and I went on our bikes to load up with mung beans, millet, bulgar, buckwheat flour and brown rice. They also sold a wonderful range of breads, including sourdoughs and pitta, which you would never find in the dear old ABC Bakers in Gloucester Road, mass-produced in the Camden Town factory.

CERES BAKERY

191 FRESTON ROAD, LONDON, W.10
PHONE 969·0819
& 269 PORTOBELLO ROAD, W.11.

RETAIL PRICE LIST

YEASTED BREADS   EFFECTIVE NOV. 3rd, 1975.

Small wholewheat, tin or round	14½p.
Large wholewheat, tin or round	22½p.
Small wholewheat stick	15½p.
Large wholewheat stick	25p.
Wholewheat rolls	4p.

Our yeasted breads are made from mature long-time doughs and are well baked to ensure there is no yeast or yeasty flavour remaining in the finished loaf.

"THE HARMONY LOAF"   14 oz ~ 17p
                          28 oz ~ 29p

The HARMONY LOAF is made with HARMONY FLOUR, a delicious mixture of wholewheat, Rye, Maize, Oat, & Barley flours.

SOURDOUGH BREADS

Large wholewheat sourdough	22½p
Small wholewheat sourdough	15½p.
Small rye, with caraway seeds	17p.
Large rye, with caraway seeds	29p

These breads combine yeasted dough with "sour" dough that has ripened for several days, developing enzymes that enhance flavour and digestibility.

NATURALLY LEAVENED BREAD 14 oz. ~ 16p.

Made entirely without yeast, this bread is sweet and very digestible.

PITA 10p. The pocket bread of the

Ceres bakery price list, 1975. (Author's Collection)

After the bland products of commercial bakeries, tasteless, glutinous and spongy, this was a revelation.

Although I knew about the Campaign for Real Ale, I didn't know that there was also a Campaign for Real Bread. This was founded in 1976 and run by the Vegetarian Society, and deserved a higher profile than it got. They were keen to expose the virtual monopoly of Spillers, Rank Hovis McDougal and Associated British Foods, who between them refined, excessively, most of the flour, mixed in all sorts of dubious additives and controlled over two-thirds of the British bread market. As it happened, the bread strike of November 1978, when 20,000 workers from the biggest bakeries stopped work over pay, did more to change habits than anything else. Local independent bakers who hadn't gone on strike had a field day, with queues round the block. People who had only eaten white, sliced bread now had to buy brown wholemeal when the white ran out, and many ended up liking it. Even in poorer areas such as Deptford, H. Hirst, Quality Baker, reported that sales of wholemeal trebled and did not decline when the strike finished, even if it cost a bit more than the cheap, white blotting paper the customers had before.

Having founded Harmony Foods and Whole Earth Foods, the Sams brothers' business boomed, and by 1976 they were employing over forty people in a huge warehouse in Willesden, shifting tons of beans and pulses every day. Then, others started to undercut their prices, and supermarkets began to climb on to the bandwagon. Greg and Craig sold up and went their separate ways, the latter founding Green & Black's organic chocolates.

One of the competitors was Neal's Yard in Covent Garden, which we discovered just a few days after it opened. There was a new fad for making your own muesli, a reaction to the sweetness and cost of the packaged Alpen, which Weetabix had started selling in the 1970s. For nuts, dried fruits and other muesli ingredients, Neal's Yard's low prices were unbeatable. Nearby in Neal Street we also stumbled upon Food For Thought, a simple and cheap vegetarian café. Their food was lentil and yoghurt based, vegetables baked with a crumble topping, chickpea casserole, carrot cake and banana bread, all extremely filling. In the crowded basement, eco-warriors in thick sweaters sat at stripped-pine tables on stools or benches. The walls were covered with notice boards plastered with small ads for acupuncture, meditation, astrology, homeopathy, naturopathy, aikido, spiritual healing and encounter groups. There was no shortage of customers seeking the alternative lifestyle.

For a while Gale, in the top-floor flat, worked at Cranks in Marshall Street and used to bring back some of their surplus stuff, chunky granary bread and couscous. Cranks didn't seem such a bad name then; people were quite pleased to be called 'cranky'. It proved to be a dated image, sold on first to Guinness, repeatedly re-branded and eventually swallowed up by Nando's.

As well as the craze for macrobiotics and vegetarianism there was an increasing awareness of where products such as rice, tea and coffee actually came from, the injustices of third-world trade, the exploitation of 'middle men' and the consequent poverty of producing countries. Following a visit to small farmers in Gujarat, India, in 1973, Richard Adams set up an agricultural import business in London, distributing to the main wholesale markets. In 1974 he started imports from Bangladesh, and set up Tearcraft and Tearfund. Traidcraft Ltd emerged out of this in 1979. All this was a welcome reaction against new concepts of TV dinners, grazing from the fridge and boil-in-a-bag Vesta meals which even in a pre-microwave era were changing social habits.

Back at the flat, with a kitchen full of pulses, beans and dried peas, augmented with fresh vegetables from North End Road, Berwick Street or any other street market which one was passing, we ate in. Geoff always seemed to have a big soup or stew simmering on the stove. As a result I didn't eat out much locally in Kensington. The exception was Daquise in Thurloe Street, just along from the awful Dino's restaurant (well, it was then) and South Kensington tube station. Recent reviewers have described this remarkable survivor as being 'stuck in the '70s'. When I first went there in 1974 it seemed to be stuck in the '50s, with a clientele of strangely dressed East Europeans whispering to each other in Slavic languages. One could imagine that they were spies swapping Cold War secrets. In fact they were mainly Poles, part of that community who'd stayed on in London after the war. The Sikorski Museum and Polish Institute were just round the corner.

A harridan, who had probably been there since the place opened in 1947, sat at a desk by the door and told you which table to take and collected your money when you left. The waitresses were young and timid. The food, however, was excellent and unusual; borszcz (beetroot soup), zrazy kasza, kolduny, golabki and bigos. Set lunch was £1.10.

Brother and sister Neil and Elspeth, living in Goodge Street, were also working part-time in the catering trade, Neil cooking galettes and pancakes in the kitchens of the newly fashionable French crêperies, Asterix and Obelix in Chelsea and Notting Hill, while Elspeth served two nights a week in the well-established Ark in Palace Gardens Terrace. The *Observer* magazine's

Daquise in Thurloe Street, 1977. (English Heritage)

review of 'Real London' in August 1977 heralded Asterix as the first place in London to do real Breton crêpes and cider. As for the Ark, it opined, 'This place keeps up high standards of plain English bistro food; value for money and nice waitresses'. Neil managed to wangle a 'background music date' for me and a pianist friend, Paddy, at the King's Road restaurant, where we thrashed our way through duets of Slavonic and Hungarian dances, all for a few quid and free crêpes.

∾ SPITALFIELDS, BRICK LANE AND CLUB ROW ∾

Having had a strong geographical bias towards North and West London, the East End was somewhere to be discovered. In my own mind, when as a child I'd been driven down the Archway or Holloway Roads in my parents' car, or later when I'd ended up there having hitched a lift to London in a lorry bound for the docks, I'd even thought of Islington as being part of the East End. I'd caught trains from Liverpool Street Station, attended rehearsals at the Arts-and-Crafts Bishopsgate Institute and drunk afterwards at Dirty Dicks, but never ventured further east.

What I had heard about, but never seen, were the great East End markets, most of which operated on Sundays because of their Jewish origins. They soon became a target for intense exploration.

Petticoat Lane, or more accurately Middlesex Street and Wentworth Street, was the most renowned, in fact probably the most famous street market in London, but I found it a disappointment. Having been given a copy of Henry Mayhew's *London Labour and the London Poor* by my Chalk Farm uncle, I'd read how Petticoat Lane had grown out of the notorious medieval second-hand cloth market known as Rag Fair, and had been described by Mayhew in 1851 as 'two or three miles of old clothes, a vista of multi-coloured dinginess'. By the 1970s all that seedy character had gone. The rag trade had moved on, and the stalls, hundreds of them, were selling standard fashion items, the same jeans, denim jackets, shirts, skirts and handbags that you could buy in Oxford Street, and at much the same price. There was nothing second-hand and nothing to rival Lawrence Corner. William Booth, founder of the Salvation Army, had disapproved of Petticoat Lane for its 'trash, cheap garments and ethnic segregation'; 'the Jew is the seller and the Gentile the buyer'. I couldn't detect any of this in 1974. Apart from Tubby Isaacs' jellied-eel stall and Bloom's kosher salt beef on Whitechapel High Street, Petticoat Lane felt as cosmopolitan as the West End.

Nor did the buildings provide an attractive backdrop for the market. On the west side a new housing estate had recently been completed, in 1975, by the City Corporation, in a harsh Brutalist style, six storeys of black brick and jutting concrete balconies. The steps up to the elevated podium opposite Wentworth Street did, however, provide a spectacular view of the multitudes below.

Trying to find an escape route from the jostling crowds of Middlesex Street by diving off into Harrow Place, I found myself in Cutler Street. There, on a tiny strip of ground known as Exchange Buildings Yard, fifty people were huddled around a row of trestle tables displaying gold coins, silver chains and medals. 'Today's prices' for gold and silver were chalked up on a blackboard. Several sinister-looking men were standing with their hands in their pockets, surveying the punters, probably minders for the stallholders on the watch for pilferers. It seemed an odd and insecure place to do such specialist and high-value business. I later found out that this whole area, once owned by the Worshipful Company of Cutlers and now lying idle, had been the headquarters and warehouses of the great East India Co. Half of Exchange Buildings Yard was cordoned off by hoardings. In 1978 comprehensive redevelopment by Greycoat Estates commenced. Some of the Georgian and Victorian buildings were saved, later to be converted by Quinlan Terry, but many were pulled down and replaced by Seifert's ten-storey offices. The biggest loss was the demolition of the magnificent 1799 warehouse which faced Middlesex Street. Exchange Buildings Yard and the gold and silver market completely disappeared.

Around the corner towards Bishopsgate was the Houndsditch Warehouse. This discount clothes store had an irritating jingle advert on local London radio, but they were true to their word, 'with hundreds of bargains just waiting for you at our store'. It beat Petticoat Lane any day.

North of Middlesex Street and Brushfield Street, Spitalfields Wholesale Fruit and Vegetable Market was a flourishing concern during the week, but closed and deserted at weekends. Unlike Covent Garden Market, the lorries weren't seen as a problem here and much of the trading was done by samples. The market was owned and operated by the City Corporation. With the imminent move of Covent Garden south-westwards to Vauxhall, there had been some talk in 1972 of moving and combining Spitalfields with the run-down Stratford Market to serve North and East London. The idea was dropped because the road connections were thought to be poor, and British Rail, the owners of Stratford, weren't the most dynamic organisation. Throughout the 1970s Spitalfields Market thrived where it was, perhaps cashing in on its central location, the only change being the contraction of the flower market and the demolition of its annex in 1978. Spitalfields attracted some big customers; even Marks & Spencer bought their fruit here.

The area east of Commercial Street was far more interesting, an extraordinary network of narrow streets lined with early eighteenth-century houses and workshops, most of which seemed to be semi-derelict. Towering above them was the steeple of Hawksmoor's Christchurch, the Portland stone caked black with soot and grime.

Up until 1970, Spitalfields and Whitechapel had been the centre of the Jewish rag trade, but the people were beginning to move out, the non-orthodox to Golders Green or Hendon, the orthodox and Hasidic to the spacious houses of Stamford Hill. Vacant properties in Spitalfields were being bought up by British Land, a major developer who was leaving them empty in anticipation of eventual comprehensive redevelopment. Meanwhile a fresh wave of immigration was flooding into the area, triggered by conflict between East and West Pakistan and the War of Independence in 1971. Bengalis, mainly men, had come to Spitalfields to work in the rag trade in the 1950s. It became an obvious magnet for Bangladeshis in the 1970s.

Many of the immigrants were excellent businessmen, and walking around the streets in 1975 there were already dozens of shops selling saris, pavadas, cholis and hijabs, and all manner of silk and cotton cloths. Food shops and restaurants blossomed, some wonderfully alluring and homely. Several times we were invited into a simply furnished back room, behind the shop, where there was a choice of meat or vegetable curry, as much as you wanted to eat for 50p.

The new community was also well organised. The Bengali Housing Action Group was formed in 1976, and in the same year the former Jewish Synagogue in Fournier Street, once a Huguenot chapel, became the new London Jamme Masjid, or mosque.

Less happily, the newcomers attracted the unwanted attention of the National Front, forerunners of today's BNP, and their ugly supporters. A vicious campaign of racist slogans and attacks culminated in the stabbing to death by three skinheads of Altab Ali, a twenty-five-year-old cloth worker in 1978. Seven thousand Bangladeshis marched behind the coffin to Hyde Park in a defiant demonstration. Such provocation served to reinforce the local community of 'Banglatown', strengthened their resolve and encouraged their leaders to become active in Tower Hamlets politics.

Brushfield Street, Spitalfields, looking towards Christchurch. (Theo Bergström)

Less immediately obvious was the other 'influx' of white middle-class or artistic pioneers, who could see the potential of these once-beautiful Georgian houses and their weavers' garrets. There had always been a few eccentrics who allegedly lived off the waste from the market, gathering fallen fruit and vegetables from the gutter and burning broken wooden pallets for heating and cooking. Now, however, there were people like Gilbert and George and Dan Cruickshank, co-founder of SAVE Britain's Heritage, who campaigned to preserve and conserve the historic buildings. In 1975 he was part of the 'sleeping-bag squad' who started squatting in an empty house in Elder Street.

They had good reason to be concerned. According to Mark Girouard, of the 230 early Georgian houses which had survived the war in Spitalfields, ninety of these had been demolished between 1957 and 1975. The Spitalfields Historic Buildings Trust was founded in 1977, and with a windfall donation from a generous benefactor, negotiations opened with British Land, the main landowners. Fortunately they abandoned their plans for comprehensive redevelopment and began to sell properties on the open market. The gentrification of Spitalfields began.

On a Sunday morning, however, our normal destination was the street market at the top end of Brick Lane, north of the railway bridge. The Truman's Black Eagle Brewery, straddling Brick Lane, had been run down following their takeover by Grand Metropolitan in 1971 and merger with Watney Mann in 1972. Most of the brewing had been moved to the expanded and modernised Stag Brewery in Mortlake. The Brick Lane buildings in 1975 seemed to be largely unused, and formed something of a no-man's-land between the bustling Bangladeshi community to the south and the market to the north. Arup's modernisation, including the rakish mirror-glass infill into the brewery yard, didn't materialise for another two years.

For anyone seeking a vision of Mayhew's London, you had to go no further than Brick Lane and Club Row Markets. Here, crammed into a series of narrow streets and derelict sites running off Brick Lane, were not only hundreds of stalls selling the full range of goods one might expect from a general retail market, but an incredibly wide cross-section of poverty and 'low-life'.

Brick Lane, and its offshoot Club Row, had the historic benefit of 'market overt'. In simple language, this allowed the casual sale of stolen goods. Put more legalistically, it allowed the buyer to acquire automatic good title to the goods, provided he/she bought them in good faith and without notice of any defect or want of title on the part of the seller. Market overt operated between sunrise and sunset, presumably so that during daylight hours goods could be sold openly and passers-by could see them. As a buyer it meant you didn't have to worry about being 'done' for handling stolen goods. For traders it meant they could get to shift stuff of doubtful provenance or which had fallen off the back of a lorry. 'These goods ain't stolen; they just ain't been paid for,' some would boast.

Nevertheless, it was always a case of 'buyer beware'. Plenty of things on offer were past their sell-by date or sub-standard. It never struck me as a good place to buy electrical goods, although plenty of people did, haggling for stereos, radios, electric toasters and televisions without knowing whether they worked properly. It wasn't always the best place to buy fresh food. On one occasion we bought a huge slab of cheddar cheese, temptingly cheap, only to find when we cut into it back in the flat that it was full of maggots inside. The contents of the buckled cans of tomatoes or kidney beans were more reliable.

The real bargains were non-perishable goods, particularly tools and ironmongery, much of which was second hand and miraculously cheap. Georgian and Victorian brass doorknobs and Art Deco bakelite handles could be bought for a song, if you were prepared to rummage through the boxes of assorted rubbish in which they lurked.

The main side turning to the west was Sclater Street, the name almost onomatopoeic for the atmosphere of the place. An elderly Jewish gentleman with a canny smile sold second-hand

Spitalfields roof tops and brewery steam, 1975. (English Heritage)

clothes from one of the railway arches on the south side of the street. There I bought my double-breasted dinner jacket and a black evening tail coat, £5 for the pair. Another man sold second-hand overalls, £1 each. Blackman's shoe shop and stall in Cheshire Street was a treasure trove, the store piled to the ceiling with cardboard boxes. Desert boots and new Doc Martens were half the price of anywhere else in London.

Everywhere there was the excited patter of salesmen, crockery sellers shouting out lower and lower prices for whole tea-sets, entrancing their audience by throwing plates high into the air and catching them. Meanwhile, pickpockets and conmen circulated among the crowds looking for unwary or gullible victims.

A patch of waste ground on Chilton Street, parallel to Sclater Street, was full of bicycles, both new and old. Most of these were probably stolen, and it was said that the real bargains went just as dawn was breaking, as soon as market overt came into operation. When Canadian Chris had his bike nicked in the West End, we went the following Sunday to try to find it at Brick Lane. Presumably because we looked like potential customers, one of the dealers invited us to visit his 'store', which turned out to be a lock-up in a North London garage court behind a block of flats. He must have thought that we didn't look like policemen. Chris and Geoff even took to buying up old bikes for £3 or £4, doing them up and selling them on at a small profit, a fairly thankless task. Most of the dealers took shortcuts, such as rubbing the rust with engine oil to make it shine.

Most of the properties in Cheshire Street were derelict, burnt out or boarded up, apparently scheduled for clearance and redevelopment by the Council. Among the ruins were several ramshackle, but cavernous, sheds where you could buy carpets, net curtains, lavatory bowls, 78s and long-playing records, and all manner of household accessories. The eastern end of Cheshire Street was a more depressing sight. Here there were rows of old men in shabby overcoats standing almost apologetically beside piles of junk, and down-and-outs holding individual items in their outstretched hands, hoping that some good Samaritan might offer a few pence for a broken watch or a chipped teapot. The western end of Bethnal Green Road was much the same, a line of the desperate and destitute sitting on the pavement trying to sell cracked cups, frayed shoes and spectacles with broken glass, the contents of someone else's dustbin.

Robert Sinclair's 1950 book on East London had described it thus: 'Nowhere else have I seen mental poverty so blindingly proclaimed... bodies and minds that lack all inner cleanliness and outer sanitation. I hope that the dying out of the older men and the civilising of the rest may lead to its disappearance before long.' Twenty-five years on, nothing much seemed to have changed. Another generation of old men had replaced the fallen.

The Club Row Animal Market was also a relic from another era which had somehow survived into the 1970s. Occupying the western section of Sclater Street, having moved south from Club Row proper on the other side of Bethnal Green Road, here were about thirty licensed pitches selling puppies, kittens, mice, hamsters and guinea pigs. There were goldfish swimming around in polythene bags, budgerigars and mynah birds in cages, tropical fish in bubbling tanks, and even snakes, newts and frogs. The sound of any barking, yelping, screeching or squawking from the animals was drowned out, not by the main road traffic but by the loudhailers and chants of protestors and demonstrators. Here too were the only policemen I ever saw at Brick Lane, presumably posted there to stop a fight. They turned a blind eye to everything else.

Animal lovers had long been campaigning to close Club Row. After a raid in 1973, the RSPCA claimed that eight out of ten animals bought at the market needed immediate veterinary treatment. Although the Tower Hamlets Council market inspectors tried to keep a close watch, the seething mass of Brick Lane made it difficult to control unlicensed hawkers and touts selling puppies from inside their coat pockets. There were tales of 'pedigree' pups dyed to the requisite colour, only for the first bath to reveal the mongrel strain. Even worse were stories of unsold kittens being thrown into litter bins when the market finished, or even sold to vivisectionists. Among the crowds there were unsavoury elements and reminders of the brutal faces of Rowlandson and Hogarth. Worse was the sight of dogs straining at their leashes, throats gurgling from the pressure, or tiny kittens in a cardboard box, heads downcast, shivering with cold and fear. The Knave of Clubs seemed an appropriate name for the pub which stood on the far side of Bethnal Green Road.

Club Row only just outlasted the '70s. The animal rights lobby won the day, and the livestock market was extinguished. Brick Lane stallholders took their place. It took much longer to reform market overt. Only with the 1994 Sale of Goods (Amendment) Act was Brick Lane brought into line with the normal law of the land.

To lift the spirits after enduring the menace and fraud in Club Row, or to celebrate the procurement of a bargain from Cheshire Street, there was the wonderful Brick Lane Beigel Bakery at the top end, open twenty-four hours a day, seven days a week (nobody had coined the phrase '24/7' in the '70s). The shop was apparently run by two brothers who did alternate twelve-hour shifts, but they got extra staff in to help with the long Sunday morning queues.

It was not far to find another Sunday-morning market that was completely different from the tumult and loafing hordes of Brick Lane. It might seem unbelievable today, but in the 1970s Columbia Road Plant and Flower Market was not widely known, and certainly not a magnet for tourists or middle-class browsers. It comprised only about twenty stalls. Run mainly by Essex market gardeners and nurserymen who sold their own produce – trays of bedding plants, garden shrubs, spring bulbs, herbs, sapling trees and cut flowers. One barrow had bags of fertiliser, and a shop called Bill and Ben sold terracotta flowerpots for the patio. In December there were Christmas trees and laurel wreaths, and one stall selling dried flowers, brightly painted teasels and pampas grass. The street was lined with two-storey terraces and lovely, unspoilt wooden shop fronts, with ordinary local shops, mostly closed on Sundays.

Above: Crockery stall, Brick Lane. (Mike Bruce)

Left: Club Row animal market. (Mike Bruce)

Parking was easy and unrestricted, and several times we used my car to collect bags of compost and plants for the balcony at Queen's Gate Terrace. Compared to Brick Lane, everyone seemed friendly and good-natured. Such a charming gem would not remain undiscovered for much longer.

∽ A SPORTING LIFE ∽

Cambridge is not a football town, never has been and probably never will be. As a child, at school and then university, the sports I'd followed had been rugby and cricket. When I came to London all the talk in the office canteen and in the pub by my colleagues and drinking mates was of football, the rivalries between the big clubs and the merits of different players. I had a lot of catching up to do.

People were incredibly loyal to their roots. In the Harrow office, Jack followed Sheffield Wednesday, while Brian supported West Ham because that's where his 'nan' lived. In the Hendon house, David was fanatical about Newcastle United, while Robin alternated his favours between Nottingham Forest and Notts County. The arguments, lubricated by many pints of beer, were prolonged.

In the Kensington flat, West Country Bryn and Canadian Geoff had even less knowledge than me about 'soccer' and no inclination to learn. Tim, however, was an avid fan of Leeds United (because his granny lived there) and 'Pompey', the club of his home town, Portsmouth. Tim was also keen to watch the real thing, so the question quickly arose as to which local club to adopt. There was always Jimmy Hill and *Match of the Day* on the television, but this had its own limitations ('for those watching in black and white, Arsenal are in red').

Chelsea was probably just the closest, but after their glory days of 1970 and 1971 the club had embarked on an over-ambitious rebuilding programme at Stamford Bridge. By 1974 they were in serious financial trouble and had sold many of their best players, such as Peter Osgood and Alan Hudson. The stadium itself was a building site and a complete mess. Worst of all were the hooligans and thugs that the club now attracted among its supporters. The whole of that part of Chelsea was worth avoiding on match days, let alone Stamford Bridge, and many local shops and pubs closed and barricaded their windows when there was a home game.

The obvious alternative was Queens Park Rangers, where a squad of excellent players had been assembled, and in 1974 Dave Sexton moved from Chelsea to be their manager. Their ground in Loftus Road, Shepherd's Bush, had been rebuilt in 1972, with the new Ellerslie Road steel-framed grandstands and terraces, smartly painted in blue. The club had not overstretched itself financially and had been able to buy fresh talent. Having got rid of the maverick Rodney Marsh, they bought the mercurial Stan Bowles, who came with the reputation of being the new George Best and soon became a folk hero. Rather like Best he had a chaotic personal life, his drinking, gambling and womanising exploits always in the papers. He was fiery tempered, ill-disciplined and didn't fit into the Alf Ramsey style, but he had immense flair. With Phil Parkes in goal, the captain Gerry Francis and John Hollins in midfield and the Irish Don Givens alongside Bowles in attack, it was the dream team, the nearest you could get in London to the 'total football' of Johan Cruyff. Thus Tim, Robin and I joined the big crowds which were being attracted to Loftus Road. We always stood in the cheap terraces among the home supporters, who were segregated from the visiting fans, particularly if it was a London derby, when up to 35,000 packed in. Outside in the streets, mounted policemen on horses were a frightening presence among the dense throng of chanting fans. One heard stories of Chelsea fans throwing glass marbles or ball bearings under the horses' hooves to make them slip.

These were heady days for QPR. In the mid-1970s Manchester United were going through a bad patch, relegated to Division Two in 1974 and beaten in the FA Cup final by lowly Southampton in 1976. Arsenal, under Terry Neill, were considered hard and dull having sold off the lank-haired Charlie George. Teams such as Ipswich, under Bobby Robson, and Derby County were better to watch. But for sheer style, none could match QPR. Tim was gutted when in April 1976 they finished runners-up by a single point in the league, especially after QPR had won thirteen and drawn one of their last fifteen games. Bill Shankly's Liverpool seemed to win everything, with David Fairclough as their 'supersub' with a knack of scoring last-gasp winning goals. Sadly it didn't last. In 1977 Dave Sexton moved on to Manchester United and things at QPR were never quite as good again.

Football was much more parochial then than it is today. There were very few non-British players. The most exotic imports into the English league were Scots like Billy Bremner or Irish like George Best. It was a sensation when in 1978 Tottenham Hotspur signed two foreign superstars, Argentinian duo Ossie Ardiles and Riccy Villa, fresh from their victory in the World Cup. After the heights of 1966 and even the 1970 World Cup, the national English football team languished in the shadow of Holland and Argentina under the cautious management of Don Revie.

The place to go and watch the 'has-beens' was Fulham. On one occasion we made the short trip down to their riverside ground at Craven Cottage and, standing among a well-mannered crowd, applauded Bobby Moore, Alan Mullery and George Best strolling through a Second Division match. At least I can say I saw them.

British rugby was in a much better state in the 1970s, with a phalanx of great players and the much-feted exploits of the Lions in New Zealand and South Africa. Gareth Edwards, Mike Gibson, Willie John McBride and David Duckham were living gods, but for me, seen only on television. With a group of the lads I went to the Varsity match at Twickenham in 1976 to see Cambridge thrash Oxford, their fifth successive victory, all faded into a blur by the pre-prandial pints in a local hostelry and the unrestrained celebrations in Richmond, which lasted long into the evening. In March these same lads went to watch the Boat Race, not that the event was much of a spectacle or the sport itself of any personal interest. As a student I had kept well clear of such hearty masochism, being too puny to row and not puny enough to cox. The real excuse was to re-acquaint oneself with the delights of the riverside Dove at Hammersmith.

The sport I watched the most and for longest was cricket, and with two Test matches each summer, at Lords and the Oval, London was the place to be. Lord's still had an old-fashioned and 'old school tie' feel. The old Tavern had gone in 1968, much lamented, but apart from the utilitarian indoor cricket school built in 1977 on the Nursery Ground, not much changed in the 1970s. 'A jumble without aesthetic aspiration, unthinkable in a country like Sweden' was how Nikolaus Pevsner had described the headquarters of cricket after the war, but then neither Swedes or Germans would have had much understanding of the epithet 'play up, play up, and play the game'. The old weather vane of Father Time still creaked above the old grandstand.

The hot summer of 1976 was much anticipated for the visit of the touring West Indies team, not least by the Caribbean community in London. Armed with a mountain of sandwiches and a couple of Party Sevens (seven-pint containers of beer), we went to the second day of the Lord's Test match, buying our surprisingly cheap £2.50 ground tickets at the turnstile in the morning. There were no restrictions on taking booze into the ground. Even the Canadians Geoff and Chris came, and enjoyed basking on the open terraces in the baking sun while being entertained by the banter from our calypso neighbours. We saw 'deadly' Derek Underwood and John Snow bowl them out for less than the England score.

It proved to be an unreliable indicator, and as the scorching summer progressed Tony Greig's boast that England would make the West Indies 'grovel' developed a hollow ring. By the time we went to the fourth day's play at the Oval in August, the slaughter was nearly over. The swaggering Vivian Richards had flayed the bowlers to every corner of the parched ground and Michael Holding (nicknamed 'Whispering Death') was now demolishing the English batting. Kennington might as well have been home soil for the West Indies and the crowd were jubilant.

The following summer we saw the Australians at Lord's on one of the few rain-affected days of another long hot summer, a season which saw the emergence of Ian Botham. For patriotic Englishmen it compensated for the trouncing of the previous summer, and the impending threat of Kerry Packer's World Series takeover.

As for my playing up and playing the game, there was the occasional Inter-Borough Planning Department football or cricket match, which took me from a suburban recreation ground in South Harrow, via a sloping mud patch on Parliament Hill, to the wide expanses of Hackney Marshes, full of seagulls and electricity pylons. Jonny had given me his Imperial College pass, which wangled me into their squash courts and swimming pool in Princes Gate, very handy and rarely busy.

Gregarious Gordon, who I'd met through music at Cambridge, was now in London working at the Bank of England and keen to share the benefits of his membership of their sports club with his friends. So attached did Gordon become to this perk that he chose to live in Kingston, much closer to the Roehampton Club than the Old Lady of Threadneedle Street. The leisure facilities were superb, the first time I'd ever had a sauna and a cold plunge, capped off by subsidised food and drink in the capacious bar, where a pint of Young's was 15p. Beyond the rugby, cricket and hockey fields was a row of immaculate grass tennis courts where Gordon and I attempted to play with enthusiasm but minimal technique. Some of our erratic shots ended up several courts away, on one occasion much to the annoyance of two rather athletic chaps, slightly more talented than us. It was Wimbledon fortnight, and they were Bjorn Borg and Vitas Gerulaitis.

∽ MARYLEBONE AND ST JOHN'S WOOD ∽

Marylebone was respectable but by no means uniformly smart in the 1970s. There were posh bits in the south towards Oxford Street, although even Harley Street, with its concentrated assortment of doctors, dentists, therapists and quacks, had a faintly seedy air. Martin, who was another musician friend from the National Youth Orchestra and Cambridge, was living in well-heeled Bryanston Square. His restrained block of flats had plush carpets in the common parts and probably service charges to match. The Wigmore Hall too had a comfortable quality and an Edwardian elegance, renamed though it was in 1917 from the original Bechstein Hall. The Wigmore attracted a fur-coated clientele, charabanced down from Golders Green, who liked to hobnob with the critics in the crowded front foyer and bar, before and after the concerts. Here I heard the wonderful Amadeus Quartet, with Norbert Brainin spinning his endless and effortless melodic lines, and the Melos Ensemble's masterly rendition of the Schubert *Octet*, etched forever into my mind. The Wigmore was widely regarded as the premiere venue for classical chamber music in London, not really challenged by the new and austere Purcell Room, but being privately run and unsubsidised it was also available for rent. It was therefore the established place where aspiring soloists with some financial backing performed debut recitals, hopefully to career-launching critical acclaim. Quality, alas, was not guaranteed. For the casual concert-goer it could be a lottery – Felicity Lott or Florence Foster Jenkins.

Most people crossed the road from the Wigmore to drink in the Pontefract Castle on the corner with Christopher Place, but those in the know wiggled up Marylebone Lane to the Golden Eagle on the corner of Bulstrode Street where clones of Russ Conway or Mrs Mills accompanied sing-songs on the honky-tonk piano. Perhaps it wasn't that unusual at the time, and no doubt there were still plenty of pub pianos and music-hall memories being re-enacted in the East End. What is remarkable is that this one pub I chanced upon has survived where others have not. Today it might be a different Mrs Mills, and there aren't so many bottles of Mackeson's stout, but the singing continues.

From the Kensington flat, we had often traversed Hyde Park to enjoy the London Pride beer in the Victoria in Stanhope Terrace or the wider range of ales in the Carpenters Arms in Seymour Place. The nearby public baths still had a steam room, one of the few still left in London. We also explored the derelict wharves and towpath of Paddington Basin, isolated and forlorn between Westway and the station. What, we wondered before we were chased away by a man with a dog, would ever happen to this wasteland? It seemed such a contrast to the elegant villas of Little Venice and the unspoilt charms of the Warwick Castle in Warwick Avenue.

North Marylebone was working class and proud of it. The tiny Beehive pub in Homer Street was a great find, with cockney humour and a beehive hair-do on the landlady. The Sea Shell fish and chip shop in Lisson Grove was cheap and excellent (pie and chips cost 15p, with fish and chips 20p), not yet tarted up or widely known. Although the up-and-coming architects Michael and Patty Hopkins had started building their exquisite new house in Downshire Hill in 1975, they hadn't yet embarked on their project in Broadley Terrace, off Lisson Grove, for their practice office.

Just round the corner was Church Street Market, which sold a huge variety of produce from Tuesday to Saturday. The western end, towards Edgware Road, was mainly fruit and veg, groceries and household hardware, crowded with locals battling it out with Irish from Kilburn, West Indians from Kensal Green, nurses from St Mary's Hospital and dossers from Paddington's red-light district. The smarter eastern half had bric-a-brac, and an increasing number of specialist shops appeared alongside Alfie's Antiques. Word had got out that there were bargains to be had, and by now the stalls thronged with Hooray Henrys from Little Venice and dealers from Portobello Road. Prices had rocketed.

Far fewer people knew about or bothered to go to Bell Street Market, just a few blocks south. We discovered it one Saturday morning in 1975 when we were looking for Bell Street Bikes, one of London's friendlier bike shops. Sprinkled along this little backwater were thirty stalls selling a strange concoction of tatty third-hand clothes, pre-war radio sets, old mangles, moth-eaten armchairs and piles of jumble. Apparently no licences were required; anyone could turn up and set out a stall. Only a handful of browsers shuffled from stall to stall, occasionally mumbling a question to a vendor. One street away the world and his wife roared along Westway, but progress and any chance of commercial success had passed Bell Street by. Even the delightfully Dickensian Greer Bookshop looked as though it hadn't sold anything for years.

On Edgware Road, the Regent Snack Bar was a relic from the 1930s, polished chrome and peach melba, and hi-fi enthusiasts like my brother scoured the electrical shops for components. Most of the newer shop fronts had garish neon and Arabic lettering.

When Tim moved from the Kensington flat to his sister's apartment above the National Westminster Bank in St John's Wood High Street, our drinking expeditions took us north. This was familiar territory, not only because of Lords. By now I was playing in a new orchestra

Carpets at Church Street Market. (Theo Bergström)

that rehearsed and performed in the beautiful St John's Wood Chapel, which stood facing the roundabout opposite the cricket ground. This conductor-less chamber orchestra was an experiment in democracy, fun but not always successful, and known by the near acronym of SWITCHCO. The inside of the church was as delightful as the exterior, and the extensions added in 1977 by Pascal and Watson were equally well done in discreet fashion. Much more eye-catching was the construction, south of the roundabout between Park Road and Regent's Park Outer Circle, of the new London Central Mosque. Foundations had started in 1972, but it took six years to finish. The architect was Frederick Gibberd, and this was his last major project and his most atypical, though arguably a counter-balance to his earlier design for 'Paddy's wigwam' (Liverpool Catholic Cathedral). The golden copper dome was an exotic contribution to the edge of the park and to Park Road, but as Bridget Cherry correctly points out in *The Buildings of England*, 'This is a place of worship and study, not another Brighton Pavilion.'

St John's Wood had some curious pubs, none more so than the Rossetti on the corner of Queen's Grove and Ordnance Hill, a post-war confection with ristorante décor and a clientele of Italian glitterati and would-be hairdressers. We went there because the landlord from Torino kept his Fuller's beer in splendid condition, and always saw us coming through the door: 'You like a pinta Prida?' The Isaac Newton and the Ordnance Arms next to the barracks seemed dull in comparison.

The Italian slant on St John's Wood was reinforced by the presence of the parental home in Acacia Road of Terry, and his alluring sisters Maxi and Fofi. Terry was a friend of Bryn, Tim and Robin from Corpus Christi, Cambridge, and a regular visitor to the Kensington flat. His father, Massimo, was a remarkable man, a quintessential Venetian who'd come to England in 1938, translated and broadcast Churchill's speeches back to Italy during the war, and set up a company importing Italian textiles into Britain. In 1978 he became president of the Italian Chamber of Commerce in the UK. Terry, meanwhile, was under pressure to work in the family business.

Neil and Elspeth left the mannequins of Goodge Street and moved into a genteel flat in Abbey Gardens, a stone's throw from the Abbey Road Studios, which was still in full swing as

St John's Wood High Street, 1977. (English Heritage)

a major recording venue. Despite the studios' fame from the Beatles' album, they had not yet become a shrine; that didn't start until the untimely death of John Lennon in 1980.

The side streets were quiet and respectable and most of the local pubs had a certain plutocratic gloom, but not the Drum and Monkey. This occupied what must have once been the living room of a house in Blenheim Terrace and was now a haven for late-night revelry and lock-ins, too good to last.

So too was Crocker's Folly in Abercorn Place. This extraordinary edifice was originally intended by the speculative builder to become the terminus hotel for the Marylebone railway, but was left stranded when the railway ended up a mile further south. The Crown Hotel was marooned in the suburbs, a sprawling feast of mahogany and marble, and for a couple of years run as a pub by the Vaux Brewery in Sunderland. It was a doomed combination.

✍ ROCK 'N' ROLL ✍

Having had a sheltered provincial childhood and a privileged but rarefied university education, my knowledge of pop culture, its music, fashion and film, was startlingly limited. Arriving in London, in order to obtain or maintain any sort of street credibility, I had to catch up fast. This included trying to gain some familiarity with parts of the 1960s which had largely passed me by, and involved participation in conversations where one had to express opinions about performers, albums and films of which I'd never heard. Various friends, including Tim, had actually been at the 1970 Isle of Wight Pop Festival, and had seen Jimi Hendrix play at 2.00 a.m. In 1970 I'd never even heard of Jimi Hendrix. A lot of bluff was required.

Jazz was easier, because I'd already listened to and liked Fats Waller, Oscar Peterson, Louis Armstrong, Dave Brubeck and Miles Davis. My school friend, Jonny, was besotted, quite understandably, with Cleo Laine and Johnny Dankworth. I went for the first time to Ronnie Scott's in Frith Street, Soho, to hear them live, with Ronnie in his pomp as the warm-up band.

Ronnie's still had a jostling, cutting-edge and an un-institutionalised informality. A student or Musicians' Union card got you in cheap. Drinks though were expensive, so it was best to get tanked up elsewhere beforehand, or try to smuggle in a hip flask or a bottle under your coat.

As a keyboard player I was more interested in jazz pianists than singers, and was readily drawn to the skills and exotic names of Thelonious Monk, Count Basie, Art Tatum and Ahmad Jamal, not that I got to see them in the flesh, relying instead on the excellent record collections of my friends and flatmates. In December 1973 I went to see Stan Tracey, one of the finest disciples of Duke Ellington, at Ronnie's. In the 1960s Tracey had been the resident pianist there, and made a name for himself with his *Under Milk Wood Suite*. Now, after a lean time when he'd considered becoming a postman, he was branching out into a more avant-garde idiom, playing alongside the likes of Keith Tippett. Soon after the 'Duke' died in May 1974, we heard Tracey playing again with Art Theman in an upstairs room above the riverside Half Moon pub in Putney.

London's jazz scene had (and still has) an off-beat and quirky feel, squeezed into strange venues, often with small but committed audiences and a casual but intense atmosphere. Sunday nights with George Melly in New Merlin's Cave in Margery Street had a louche steaminess which drew the crowds, as did Humphrey Lyttleton at the Old Bull at Barnes.

Two friends of Geoff in the Kensington flat were enthusiastic followers of Chick Corea and his more adventurous style. Pete and Juliet lived in a succession of scruffy, smoke-filled flats in Brixton, Compton Terrace, Islington, and Frederick Street, near King's Cross, but through the weedy haze they introduced me to the mesmeric magic of Keith Jarrett. His solo album *Facing You* and the recording of his famous Köln concert of January 1975 were a revelation. When, eventually, our young hero (aged thirty-two) came to perform in London at the Hammersmith Odeon in October 1977, we were there among the adoring fans, swept away and entranced by his complete immersion into his own cocoon of improvisation, his stamina and his idiosyncratic mannerisms of grunting, crooning and standing at the keyboard.

The eclectic range of Bryn's record collection included plenty of mainstream pop and rock music – but no Abba I hasten to add. The huge surge of British hard rock, heavy rock, blues rock, psychedelic rock and heavy metal from the 1970s were well represented with Deep Purple, Pink Floyd, Status Quo and Black Sabbath, but art and glam rock were most favoured in the Queen's Gate Terrace flat. Roxy Music with Bryan Ferry, Andy Mackay and Brian Eno, Freddie Mercury and Queen and 10cc were the most played, and their eye-catching record covers the most drooled over. 'Bungalow ranch-style, open-plan living' became a common catchphrase in the flat.

Prized items were the weird and wonderful albums of Frank Zappa and his Mothers of Invention and Captain Beefheart and his Magic Band. When the opportunity arose, as with Keith Jarrett, we eagerly crammed into the Odeon to hear Zappa strut his stuff. Alongside Hunter S. Thompson's *Fear and Loathing in Las Vegas*, Zappa encapsulated the anti-establishment and anarchic reaction against corporate capitalist America. 'Webcore' and 'Great Bats' summed up the lunacy of it all.

London, meanwhile, was full of new music venues: the Mean Fiddler in Willesden, the Hope and Anchor and George Robey in Islington, and the Electric Ballroom, Music Machine and Dingwalls in Camden. These began to rival the established halls such as the Rainbow at Finsbury Park and the Roundhouse at Chalk Farm, both of which hit troubled times in the 1970s. At the Rainbow there were concerns about public safety, particularly the structural capacity of the wide-open balcony with hundreds of people jumping up and down in unison.

Several bands consciously cultivated and encouraged lewd behaviour and acts of wanton destruction. Led Zeppelin, with Jimmy Page, probably led the way, described in the mid-1970s as 'the biggest band in the world', known as much for riding motorbikes down hotel corridors and 'feasting on fourteen-year-old groupies and spitting out the bones', as for their most famous track, 'Stairway to Heaven'. Album sleeves such as *Houses of the Holy* were intentionally sensational and apocalyptic. They arguably wrote the bible of bad taste which all others followed. Punk was no more than a natural progression, and while Johnny Rotten and the Sex Pistols caused an outbreak of official moral pandemonium with their *God Save the Queen* in 1977, the Jubilee year, it had all been done before. When Ian Dury and the Blockheads produced their 'Sex and Drugs and Rock and Roll' track in the same year, it had a certain tongue-in-cheek irony. There were exceptions to such anarchy, such as Bryan Ferry, who in his Zorro and tuxedo outfits was nicknamed 'Byron Ferrari', 'more likely to redecorate a hotel bedroom than trash it'.

The fashion for extremes was equally evident in the crossover between music, film and fashion. Stanley Kubrick's *A Clockwork Orange*, Sam Peckinpah's *Straw Dogs* and Ken Russell's *The Devils*, all released in 1971, were shocking at the time for their depiction of gratuitous violence. *A Clockwork Orange*, with its thugs and droogs, was withdrawn by the censors in 1974 on the basis that it might inspire copycat crime. Cinemas which premiered William Friedkin's *The Exorcist* in 1974 reportedly had higher cleaning bills following the revulsion of many of their audiences who were physically sick in the auditorium or toilets during some of the more explicit scenes.

After his success with *Women In Love*, Ken Russell was at his most prolific in the '70s, producing a string of extravagant films such as *The Music Lovers*, *Savage Messiah* and *Lisztomania*, all very much in the spirit of the age, but none more so than *Tommy*. I'd heard their 1973 album *Quadrophenia*, but sitting in the Paris Pullman cinema in Drayton Gardens in 1975, shortly after *Tommy* was released, was the first time I'd seen The Who, Roger Daltrey et al. The pin-ball

Busking with Bryn in Bruges.
(Author's Collection)

wizard and the baked beans certainly left a lasting impression, more than can be said for David Essex in *Godspell* or *Stardust*, both of which I sat through. I have to confess that even David Bowie's *The Man Who Fell to Earth* left me cold, despite its surrealism and cult following.

I did manage to see *The Rocky Horror Show*, but not with Julie Covington and Tim Curry from the original cast. That had opened in 1973 in the Theatre Upstairs at the Royal Court in Sloane Square but transferred via the Classic cinema to the nearby Kings Road Theatre in November 1973, where it ran until the threat of demolition in 1979. By the time the Paris Pullman was demolished in 1980, Chelsea and Kensington had lost a lot of its old cinemas.

The Paris Pullman was a particular loss. Together with the Everyman in Hampstead and the Academy in Oxford Street, with its elderly usherettes, it was the best place to see the latest art-house films, whatever took your fancy from Bunuel to Bergman. The Paris Pullman was handy for the Kensington flat, and is where I saw *Blanche*, *The French Connection*, *A Touch of Class* and *The Discreet Charm of the Bourgeoisie*.

General-release Hollywood films were shown at the big cinemas, still non-multiplexed in the 1970s, and seemingly in terminal decline, as people preferred to sit at home and watch their new colour televisions. Cinema attendance plummeted in the 1970s and it might have been worse. Fortunately, not many films were made for or shown on television (Steven Spielberg's *Duel* was a notable American exception), nor were there readily available videos or DVDs. If you wanted to see the latest cult film such as *Annie Hall*, *The Day of the Jackal*, *The Outlaw Josey Wales*, *Star Wars* or *The Deer Hunter*, you had to go to the cinema.

Video-cassette recorders had been introduced by Sony, Philips and Grundig in the early 1970s but cost about £600, an absolute fortune then. Better models such as the Philips Video 2000 were not marketed until 1979, but they still weren't cheap. Television, meanwhile, consisted of just three channels, BBC1, BBC2 and ITV. A new one, Channel 4, was planned but didn't open until 1982. All three channels were by now in colour at least, not that we had a colour television in the flat.

With so much music to listen to, copious mung beans to be munched and many pints of beer to be drunk, we watched the box very little. Much was eminently avoidable; the achingly dull *Dixon of Dock Green* or *Z Cars*, but I missed seminal productions such as Dennis Potter's *Pennies From Heaven*. Unmissable were the 1974 episodes of *Monty Python*, the subsequently brilliant series of *Ripping Yarns* and the excruciatingly funny *Fawlty Towers*. Together with the films of *Monty Python and the Holy Grail*, *Jabberwocky* and *The Life of Brian*, they provided our richest vein of humour. Brave Sir Robin and the Knights of Ni were rarely off our lips. Barry Humphries and Barry Crocker offered raunchier and more puerile merriment in their Barry Mackenzie films, with raw prawns and one-eyed trouser snakes. Rather like Derek and Clive, it was best to keep girlfriends and grannies away from this stuff, although the *Edna Everage Housewife Superstar* show, which we all went to see at the Globe Theatre, had universal appeal.

The strongest influence of music and cinema on everyday life was how we dressed and wore our hair. For young men it was flares, bell-bottoms or loons, dangerous enough to get tangled up in bicycle chains, and shirts with huge collars, lapels and cuffs, Edwardian frock coats, frills and ruffs, or Army surplus great coats. The ostentatious, strutting like popinjays, wore velvet trousers, snake-skin jackets and high-heeled boots with platform soles, winkle pickers or hush puppies. Colour co-ordination was derided, certainly to be avoided. Hair was grown long, either bouffant and combed like Kevin Keegan or unkempt like Charles Manson, with as much facial hair, sideburns, beards or moustaches as you could muster. Older men, or those needing a more mature look, fashioned themselves on Alan Bates, Oliver Reed and Donald Sutherland.

... like it needs another plague. Punks at Swiss Cottage. (Theo Bergström)

From *A Clockwork Orange*, aided and abetted by the bohemian rhapsody of Freddie Mercury, came the influence of eye make-up, braces, bowler hats and bovver-boots. From the skinhead came the progression to punk and grunge. The Sex Pistols and the Clash threw away their flares and cheesecloth and donned drainpipe jeans, ripped T-shirts and leather ties. Their fans such as the Bromley Contingent followed suit. Tattoo and piercing shops sprung up all over the seedier parts of London. In the King's Road, Vivienne Westwood and Malcolm McLaren, manager of the Sex Pistols, opened their up-market punk fashion shop, Sex.

For most women the freedom of expression was perhaps less extreme; fewer birds of paradise perhaps than the masculine peacocks. Some adopted the Laura Ashley-style of floral patterns and Victorian over-decoration. Others drifted around London dressed as Gothic milkmaids in diaphanous dresses, or more rustically in smocks and dungarees. Some modelled themselves on the summery softness of Julie Christie who, in *Don't Look Now* and *The Go Between*, had caught the eye as a successor to Joan Bakewell's 'thinking man's crumpet'. Al Pacino called her 'the most poetic of all actresses'.

Liberated from the sensible shoes of school days, women wore everything from knee-high boots to exotic open-toed sandals with long ribbon laces tied around the ankles. The eco-warriors wore multi-coloured, home-knitted jumpers and baggy trousers, or overalls, espadrilles, clogs or Doc Martens. In a decade of excess, it was un-cool to be cool.

✧ BAROQUE 'N' DRUM ROLL ✧

Having been a small fish in a medium-sized pond in Cambridge, I swam into the enormous ocean of London with a degree of apprehension. It quickly became apparent that the shortage of bassoon players in Cambridge was replicated in London, and I was soon being invited to join more orchestras, groups and bands than I could sensibly manage with a daytime job.

In the spring of 1973 I was asked to play in Chelsea Opera Group, who were giving concert performances of Puccini's *Turandot* in Fairfield Hall, Croydon, Oxford Town Hall and Cambridge Guildhall. Nicholas Braithwaite conducted and Valerie Hill and Geoffrey Shovelton sang Turandot and Calaf with commanding effect. Chelsea Opera Group was already a long-established institution, having been founded in 1950 by the musicologist David Cairns, and a considerable number of the players seemed old enough to have been founder members. All the rehearsals were in Lincoln's Inn, which perhaps contributed to my initial impression of a somewhat staid and mature organisation. Nevertheless I was asked back to do more series, including *Rusland and Ludmilla*, and in March 1975 for their twenty-fifth anniversary concert performance of *Fidelio* in St John's Smith Square, conducted by Colin Davis.

Not that every operatic experience was so glamorous. In October 1973 I agreed to deputise for a Friday evening performance of *Fledermaus* in Ruislip. I arrived in good time for the 7.30 p.m. start, but was alarmed to find the car park at the back of the Winston Churchill Hall full to overflowing and the stage door firmly locked. In the front foyer I discovered that the show had begun at 7 p.m. with the overture in full swing. The only way to the orchestra pit was to walk down the central aisle, past the audience, and to climb over the rail and through the other players to find my seat in the woodwind. The £3 fee did not compensate for the embarrassment.

Surprisingly my copybook was not blotted. I was booked to play for both John Lewis Opera and Gemini Opera in Richmond. When their Oxford Street store was rebuilt in 1960, John Lewis incorporated a theatre, and the annual autumn in-house opera productions were a much-valued part of the social life of the partnership, with the staff actively encouraged to participate. The orchestra were ringers, paid quite handsomely for two weeks of rehearsals and performances, every night packed with loyal supporters of the brave souls on stage.

Gemini Opera enjoyed the cosy charms of the delightful Richmond Theatre, where Nick Conran wielded an amiable baton and much lubrication was taken in the Cricketers before and after the shows. The trumpeter, Peter Boakes, thoughtfully provided the whoopee cushion that was slipped onto the chair of the leader before he sat down after taking his bow.

As for amateur orchestras, London was awash with them. For a brief time I was lured into the Hackney Orchestra, conducted by Peter Susskind, son of the eminent Walter. Their concerts in Hackney or Stoke Newington Town Halls were sparsely attended by a variety of tramps and vagrants, some of whom probably quite enjoyed the sounds we made, and some of whom contributed sounds of their own. The Barbican Orchestra was even more bizarre, starting life as the Civil Service Orchestra and receiving adult-education funding from the Central London Institute. Its director was David Thompson, a principal violin in the orchestra of the Royal Opera House and a fine musician, but a fallible organiser and an erratic and perspiring conductor. Rehearsals, usually held in the Hugh Myddelton School in Clerkenwell (then part of Kingsway College), were ill-disciplined and shambolic, often completely lacking a brass section or double basses. It almost justified the old and scurrilous 'What's the difference between a cow and an orchestra?' joke. ('The cow has the horns at the front and the … at the back'.) Somehow, however, he enticed the great John Pritchard to conduct a concert in March 1974 in aid of the Musicians' Benevolent Fund, miraculously extracting a sterling rendition of Rachmaninov's *Second Symphony* out of the motley ensemble. My final appearance was in a hopelessly ambitious operatic evening, with excerpts from *Die Meistersinger*, *Tristan and Isolde* and *Boris Godunov*, conducted by Thompson himself. Despite an orchestra of over eighty, there were only six people in the audience. 'Fats', as we called him, was seen downing four pints of beer in the interval, drowning his sorrows, and he slumped at the rostrum in the second half with his bow tie undone and one hand in his pocket. Not long after that, the orchestra folded.

The Salomon Orchestra was a better bet, commonly regarded as the outstanding offer for amateurs in 1970s London. This orchestra had been formed in 1963 by Nicholas Braithwaite, among others, and attracted a younger set of players than the Chelsea Opera Group and of a higher standard. Even better, it booked the rising stars of the conducting world, not only Braithwaite and John Elliot Gardiner, but the youthful Simon Rattle. I had remembered him as a precocious brat in the National Youth Orchestra but now in 1974, aged nineteen, he was already assistant conductor of the Bournemouth Symphony Orchestra and mature beyond his years. Simon seemed to have a rare gift, almost a sixth sense. It wasn't just that he unerringly knew the name of everyone in the orchestra, but he sensed the potential and capability of each player, getting the best out of every individual to serve the common good of the orchestra. Rattle's performances of Mahler's *Das Lied von der Erde* and his *Sixth Symphony*, Nielsen's *Fourth Symphony* and Richard Strauss' *Don Quixote* with Moray Welsh were more than memorable, and it was a privilege to have been part of it.

The orchestra was well organised and efficiently managed by Oliver Taylor. The concentrated sessions of rehearsals were held in varied venues such as City University in St John Street, Cardinal Vaughan School in Shepherd's Bush or Baden Powell House, very handy for my Kensington flat. Trinity Church Square, where Holy Trinity had been gutted by fire in 1973 and converted in 1975 by Arup Associates into an orchestral recording and rehearsal space, was the most enjoyable. Best of all there were usually two or three out-of-town performances at places such as Stowe, Charterhouse and Christ's Hospital schools, or Turner Simms Hall, Southampton, and the Gardner Arts Centre in Sussex, used as warm-ups before the London concert in St John's Smith Square.

In Salomon I met and made a whole new circle of friends. Paddy and Di Clements, the Maries twins Al and Keith, Betty Shipp and Wynn Hart, Peter and Ann Wiggins, Colin and Anita Beak

Frank Shipway, 1976. (Clive Barda)

The Great Hall and concert venue, Altenburg Monastery, Austria, 1974. (Author's Collection)

and Jeremy Polmear were a close-knit group, mostly a few years older than me, and full of *joie de vivre*. Some had been at Cambridge, others not, but were pursuing a variety of professional careers. Colin was an acoustician, the brains behind the mushrooms suspended from the ceiling of the Albert Hall, and an enthusiast for sports cars, one of which bore the number plate BAS 500N.

Salomon more than made up for the demise of the East Anglian Symphony Orchestra, which I had continued playing in from my university days. Its swansong had been in November 1974, first an excellent concert in Snape, followed by a disastrous repeat in the Theatre Royal, Bury St Edmunds, where the alcoholic farewell party was given before the concert; not good for precision in Stravinsky's *Dumbarton Oaks*!

A rival to Salomon in its own inimitable way was Forest Philharmonic, founded in 1964 and directed by the indomitable Frank Shipway. Forest Phil was based exclusively in Walthamstow, generously funded by Langham Life Assurance and the London Borough of Waltham Forest, rehearsing like clockwork every Monday evening in the North East London Polytechnic on Forest Road to justify its evening class status, and giving their concerts in the Assembly Hall next door, five each year and always on a Sunday night. Shipway's reputation went before him and when I was called by his secretary, Sue Rivers, as a potential new principal bassoon and invited to visit his house in Chelwood Gardens, Richmond, to play for him, I did so with some trepidation. I was not disappointed when he opened the door wearing a velvet smoking jacket and puffing on a huge Cuban cigar.

Frank Shipway modelled himself unashamedly on his hero and mentor, Herbert von Karajan, not only the black polo-neck jumpers, the sweater draped over the shoulders and the gelled, slicked-back hair (probably dyed), but the whole gamut of Karajan mannerisms, even at times a fake German accent despite his Brummy origins. Behind the façade was something more akin to a Teddy boy. Before one concert with the Hatfield Philharmonic (which Frank also conducted), I was a soloist in the Mozart *Sinfonia Concertante* and was sharing a dressing room with Frank. He waltzed in wearing a long black cloak, from beneath which he produced a large bottle of Pepsi Cola. Frank drove a Jaguar, rather than a Mercedes.

His musical interpretation was pure Karajan, woodwind parts doubled, notes bulged and squeezed. The sets of orchestral parts were heavily annotated in red ink, each note marked with lines, slurs, accents and extreme dynamics. For those without thick skins the sectional rehearsals could be an unsettling experience, where he would unerringly pick on the weak and nervous to play on their own. Any protestation would be met by the response, 'Your technical problems do not concern me, boy'. Such bullying did not suit everyone, and many good players upped sticks. Nor was there much chance for fraternising or plotting among the players. Rehearsals started at 7.30 p.m. and finished at 10.30 p.m. on the dot, purposefully after pub closing time in outer London, not that the Double Diamond in the Bell on Forest Road was any great loss. In any event, it was a bleak part of town, miles from a tube or Underground station, and a hell of long drive from Kensington. It was difficult to skive off rehearsals. Occasionally double-booked and feigning illness, I had to prime and bribe my flat mates to say the right thing when a minion made the inevitable phone call to check up.

Yet despite the tyranny, I stuck at it for two years. For the concerts the strings were stiffened by various hardened old pros from the BBC Symphony Orchestra and the Philharmonia. Arthur Price was a reliable leader who got the band out of a few difficult corners. Frank excelled at the big romantic block-busters, and Mahler's *Third* and *Fifth Symphonies*, Tchaikovsky's *Fourth* and Rachmaninov's *Symphonic Dances* were electric. The *Rite of Spring* was beyond him, and his Mozart and Haydn verged on bad taste.

The constraints imposed by conductors was a frequent topic of discussion, and a direct result of this was the founding of the conductor-less St John's Wood Chamber Orchestra, previously mentioned, by the oboist Jeremy Polmear, his pianist partner Di Ambache and the violinist Paul Collins. Paul was a gruff Canadian and a fine fiddle player who had led the Royal Liverpool Philharmonic and now was freelance in London. He happened also to be a drinking chum of my Chalk Farm uncle in the Rosslyn Arms, Hampstead. He had become the regular leader of Salomon, with a reliably grumpy attitude towards misguided authority.

Another democratic musical venture was the long-running project to play through all 104 of Haydn's symphonies, probably a pioneering example of the cycles and music marathons which subsequently became all the rage. On several happy occasions I was asked along for a Sunday at Peter Collins' rural retreat in leafy Hertfordshire, the Coach House to the magnificent Tudor Standon Lordship, where the assembled group would tackle three or four symphonies before indulging in Joy Collins' wonderful food and Peter's lively homemade beer.

Better still was the prospect of chamber music. In big orchestras, bassoons are often drowned out by the heavy brass, and even in smaller bands they frequently double up with the cellos and basses. In chamber music, every note you played really counted. In the autumn of 1973 I'd signed up at Morley College, Waterloo, for the Saturday morning wind band, which placed a strong emphasis on contemporary repertoire. It was run by Michael Graubart, one of several pre-war East European and German refugees who'd gravitated towards the college, most famously the Hungarian Matyas Seiber. Another was Wally Wurtzburger, composer and conductor of the Kingston Philharmonia, and a keen and willing second bassoonist in the wind band. At the time the place was a building site, as the contractors raced to finish the new extension in time for the Queen's visit on 10 December. The wind band was picked to provide the royal welcome and the choice of Stravinsky's *Symphonies of Wind Instruments* was perhaps not the jolliest fanfare. Nor do I know what she made of John Winter's spectacular architecture, all smooth brown aluminium and tinted glass.

A more exciting but short-lived adventure was the formation with various friends of a wind octet, which we rather pompously called the London Woodwind Ensemble (LWE). Like many of our generation we were inspired by the superb new recordings of the Netherlands Wind Ensemble. The two clarinettists, David Campbell and Mike Penny, managed to persuade Thea King to coach us, both in the Royal College of Music and at her house in Milverton Road Brondesbury, and we surprisingly won a London and South East competition for young musicians, rewarded by concerts in the Fairfield Hall, the Blackheath Concert Hall and the Bloomsbury Collegiate Theatre in the summer of 1974.

When the LWE faltered, the Whispering Wind Band took its place. This was run by the oboist Jeremy Polmear, and was similarly a wind octet but enhanced by the provision of lots of good arrangements by his friend, Roger Calkwell, of Beatles songs and Scott Joplin rags (suddenly universally popular as the 1973 sound track from *The Sting*). We rehearsed at Exeter Road, Kilburn, near my brother's flat, and in the Holy Cross Church in Cromer Street, King's Cross, before launching on a series of open-air concerts. The first of these was in Camden Lock on a Saturday morning in June 1974, when the newly-fledged market was packed with hippies and students, including my brother and his Friends of the Earth buddies. The Greater London Council Arts Department provided some money for us to play in the bandstands of Golders Hill Park, Waterlow Park and Cherry Tree Wood in Highgate. We also did a date in the pizzeria in the old dairy in Coptic Street, Bloomsbury, home of the first Pizza Express. The wind octet was too loud as background music, and probably deafened most of the punters. The management reverted to their preferred formula of string quartets.

By now my Cambridge school friend John Richens was in London working as a house doctor at King's College Hospital in Denmark Hill. Under the auspices of the Medical College Student Union, he organised regular lunchtime concerts in the Nurses' Recreation Room, during which we worked our way through most of the piano duet repertoire in front of small but enthusiastic audiences.

Music certainly took me to places I might otherwise not have gone: the Great Hall of St Bartholomew's Hospital, the Orangery at Holland Park, and St Alfege's Church and the Royal Naval College Chapel in Greenwich with the Tallis Chamber Choir, the latter for a performance of Monteverdi's *Vespers*, through which Prince Philip slept soundly in his front row seat, much to the discomfort of Richard Baker who was compèring the evening and sitting beside him.

Music also took me out of London, with Tallis and Philip Simms to Westleton in Suffolk and with John Elliot Gardiner to Fontmell Magna in Dorset. There were one-off choral society dates, the Wooburn Singers with Richard Hickox in High Wycombe or Guildford Cathedral with Nick Steinitz. The young architect and bassoonist Rick Griffiths organised concerts at Great Maytham Hall in Kent and Aynho Park in the Cotswolds, both of which were being converted with his involvement into flats by the Country Houses Association.

Another one-off, for me at any rate, was Music Camp at Piggotts in the Chilterns. This former home of Eric Gill had been bought in the 1960s by Bernard Robinson, a physicist and keen amateur musician who had been running music camps elsewhere since the 1920s. It occupied a beech-ringed hill top with a micro-climate all of its own; wet, windy and cold and, worse still, seemingly miles from the nearest pub. The old flint and brick farmhouse had a certain charm, with a few bits of Eric Gill pottery and sculpture dotted about, but the corrugated iron barns and outbuildings were less attractive. The whole place had a flavour of Boy Scouts, with an above-average smattering of eccentric and bossy men wearing baggy shorts. My weekend was spent hacking through Harrison Birtwhistle's 1971 orchestral tone-poem, *The Triumph of Time*. It was more like a triumph of slime. I wasn't keen at digging latrines, peeling potatoes for fifty people or being a breakfast monitor in charge of reveille, or singing madrigals in the narthex after evening cocoa. Camping and music making, I decided, good as they both were, didn't mix.

There were trips to Oxford to play in the Apollo Orchestra, run by the indefatigable Frances Royals, for a weekend of rehearsals in the Dragon School or Netherswell Manor. This was followed by a concert on the Sunday evening in the Polytechnic up on Headington Hill (now Oxford Brookes University) or Oxford Town Hall, always in aid of the Malcolm Sargent Cancer Fund for Children. Frankie and her tireless father, who spent all his time ferrying people to and from railway stations, assembled a star-studded band of young professionals and amateurs. The baby faced Bradley Creswick was leader and the regular conductors were Andrew Massey, before he went off to be assistant to Lorin Maazel with the Cleveland Orchestra, and Antony Beaumont, before he went to live in Germany. The ultimate highlight was Felicity Lott in a backless dress singing Richard Strauss' *Four Last Songs* in September 1977. Much was drunk afterwards in the Bear.

The Hertfordshire Chamber Orchestra was another chance for weekends in the country, rehearsing in Aldwickbury Prep School near Harpenden during their holidays, sleeping in the dorms, and giving a pair of concerts the following weekend in Hertfordshire and London. Most of the players, even if they had once had local connections, now lived in London. Here was an introduction to another new circle of friends: Gordon and Janie, Julie and Cathy, Peter and Jim Smith, Dale and Keith, Gabriel and Jessica, Clive and Jane, and a quartet of horn players, Robin, Jonathan, Roger and Mark, a completely different set from Salomon. There were woodland walks on the free Saturday afternoons, country pubs after rehearsals, games of round-the-table-tennis and late-night dips in the school swimming pool.

Even better were the trips abroad. In August 1974, conveniently coinciding with my state of homelessness, I was asked to participate in an international music festival in Austria run by Maeve and Gunther Auer. She was an excellent violinist, he an ambitious conductor, and they lived at a smart address in Ladbrooke Gardens. The journey to Vienna by train from

The author sandwiched between Andrew Marriner and Robin O'Neill, 1978. (Dick Makin)

Victoria took twenty-four hours, followed by three hours on a bus to the remote town of Horn, only twenty miles from the Czechoslovakian border in the sector of Austria which had been occupied by the Russians. The multi-national orchestra members were put up in Schloss Breiteneich, while the concerts were given in the magnificent baroque Benedictine monastery of Altenberg, where there was still a large community of monks who cultivated their vegetables and venison and brewed their own beer. We ate and were served by them in their refectory. During and after the war, when the abbey served as a garrison for the Red Army, some of the illiterate soldiers had burnt many of the precious books in the library to keep warm, apparently including several manuscripts by Haydn and Schubert. From the elevated perch of the terraces there were views of rolling hills and wooded valleys, inhabited by wild boar. After Hendon and Harrow, it was a step back in time, a history lesson come alive.

Just two weeks later I set off for Ibiza with an orchestra that was being managed by Di Clements, comprising string players from the English Chamber Orchestra, led by Jurgen Hess, and wind players, mainly from Salomon, including Di's husband Paddy. The conductor was an American, Gene Forrell, whose daughter was a near neighbour of Paddy and Di in Tavistock Terrace, Holloway, and the trip was attractively remunerated, bank-rolled by a generous Californian millionaire, Don Traub.

Ibiza was, in 1974, still a part of Spain ruled by Franco, largely unspoilt and undeveloped apart from our nearly completed hotel at the end of the airport runway. The rehearsals and outdoor concerts were in the courtyard of the castle at the top of the old town. In between the five concerts of all-Mozart there was jazz, with Pete King and Roland Kirk and his Vibration Society, who were also staying at our hotel. Kirk was a remarkable multi-instrumentalist, blind almost from birth, but somehow able to play several saxophones or flutes simultaneously to extraordinary effect. The audience was spellbound by all four of his concerts. Neil and I on bassoon had an easy time of it, a tour to remember, not least for Don Traub's voluptuous daughters. Sadly it never happened again, or if it did we weren't invited. A later trip to play for Gene Forrell at Wolverton Manor Shorewell was pleasant enough, enjoying goose eggs for breakfast courtesy of our hosts the Pattersons, but the Isle of Wight wasn't quite so exotic.

Foreign forays prospered, however, with the Hertfordshire Chamber Orchestra, where their new conductor, Howard Williams, had good contacts with the Flanders Festival. The visit to Bruges in August 1978 proved to be the first of many to Belgium and an introduction to its fine strong beers, at the time unknown and unavailable in London. The lethal strength of Duval and Trappist triples finally taught me the lesson that it was not a good idea to drink before playing. When the legendary trumpeter John Wilbraham was once asked how he managed to play after drinking, 'Jumbo' had retorted, 'Well, I practise when I'm drunk'. I, fortunately, did not have quite his constitution.

∽ ISLINGTON ∽

The downside of moving to the flat in Kensington was my journey to work in Harrow. It had been far enough from Hendon, but now it really was un-cycleable, a horrific and exhausting marathon attempted only once. Public transport was slow and expensive, so I used my Morris Minor. The gypsy encampment beside the motorway at White City, the Guinness Brewery at Park Royal and the endless road works at Hanger Lane roundabout became familiar landmarks.

The solution was to find a new job, and fortunately I didn't have to wait long. In December 1974 I replied to an advertisement in the *Municipal Journal* for an urban designer job in the Planning Department of the London Borough of Islington. I went for an interview in early February, had a medical at the Highbury Grange Health Centre in April, and eventually started work on 2 June 1975, little expecting that I would be there for the next thirty-two years.

I already knew a few little pockets of Islington. A cousin lived in a squalid flat in a semi-derelict house in Offord Road, and a clarinet-playing friend from Cambridge was lodging in St Paul's Road. We'd met for a drink in the grotty Alwyne Castle pub. Meanwhile, Geoff from the Kensington flat had started working part-time in the Musicians' Union office at the junction of Colebrooke Row and Noel Road, where the Island Queen was a delightful and irresistible attraction with its Charrington's beer and fantasy creatures suspended from the high ceilings.

The Planning Department offices were at Nos 227-229 Essex Road on the corner with Canonbury Street, just along from the busy junction with Canonbury Road and New North Road. The building, next to the Polytechnic's School of Librarianship, was a rambling 1920s former shirt factory, inconveniently laid out over four floors which were connected by goods lifts with heavy concertina gates and steep narrow flights of stairs. Compared to the modern and blandly corporate Civic Centre at Harrow it had a quirky charm. At the back of the ground floor was a large covered garage with a dodgy glazed roof. The chief planner, Ken Blythe, and his deputy Bert Newbrook occupied the small top floor, the eagles' nest as we called it, with their secretary May Moore. Blythe was an elusive figure, always on the golf course, some people said, or driving there in his Jag, and I only spoke to him once before he retired in 1976. He died soon after.

My first impression of Islington, not only the immediate environment of the office in Essex Road but also Upper Street, the Angel and the backstreets, was one of drab ordinariness. The main roads were lined with run-of-the-mill local shops catering for mainly working-class residents. The parade opposite the office, occupying the ground floor of Bentham Court, included Goodwin's butchers, Ferris fishmongers, Barton's the bakers, Lipton's grocers, Spivack the chemist, and a Post Office. Further up towards Islington Green was Vinn's bakers, preferable to Barton's because of the cheery dears who sold slabs of bread pudding and Belgian buns at rock-bottom prices, and called you 'ducky' for your pains. Aston Matthews opposite was a basic builders' merchants, not the fancy bathroom showroom it is today. Heal's furniture factory occupied two large sites on the north-west side of Essex Road between Gaskin Street and Dagmar Terrace, while next to the Green itself was the sprawling Anderson's timber yard, which had also expanded onto a site at the corner of St Peter's Street and Colebrooke Row. Only one retailer was showing an interest in the more affluent minority. Steve Hatt had been to Highgate School and when he inherited the prosperous family fishmonger business opposite the end of Cross Street, he had an eye to new clientele and the future.

Going the other way along Essex Road towards Newington Green, Jays the jeweller was on its last legs behind its splendid Edwardian frontage. Less splendid were the shop fronts and garish signage of the Sultan Ahmet and Doner Kebab house, which offered cheap Turkish food where you could take in your own wine without paying corkage. We called it the Sultan's Armpit.

Upper Street was equally ordinary, with only a couple of estate agents, Prebble's and Stickley & Kent, and a smattering of greasy-spoon cafés scattered amongst work-a-day local shops. Benson's at No. 70 and Guardian Travel at No. 87 competed for business. Robertson's Tools at No. 120, Blackman's hardware at No. 151, Stevens butchers at No. 179, Smokes tobacconist at No. 204 and the Canonbury Bookshop at No. 268 were all long-established businesses. The Midland Bank had a branch on the corner with Waterloo Place, opposite the police station. The pubs still had their original names, the Fox, the Pied Bull, the Old Parr's Head, the Shakespeare, and the Angel and Crown. In the coaching yard behind the Hare and Hounds and in other side alleys were car-repair workshops and small factories. The nearest thing to a supermarket was Key Markets at No. 213.

Only Camden Passage had any real buzz to it, where the antiques and bric-a-brac market which had been set up in the 1960s was hugely successful and attracted crowds of visitors on Wednesdays and Saturdays. Older businesses were under pressure here, such as Levey's sewing machines and Peck's toy shop. The demand for more stalls saw the conversion of the derelict tram shed on Islington High Street into an antiques arcade. Frederick's and Carrier's restaurants catered for the fatter wallet, while Aquilino's and the wonderful Alfredo's were cheaper. There was some excitement when Monsieur Frogs replaced the dingy Harlequin restaurant at No. 31 Essex Road in 1976 and the Roxy Diner opened in Upper Street. The arrival of Bread & Roses' whole food shop at No. 316 was also a sign of things to come. By 1979 Marsdens Wine Lodge, After Dark and a new Baskin Robbins ice-cream parlour were offering more competition. Brew-it-Yourself was a new homebrew shop and Pickering's dentists had opened, together with Rising Free and The Other Bookshop. Things were beginning to change.

The Angel junction and the properties all around it were still blighted and run down, despite the Herculean endeavours of the highly active and articulate Islington Society who, with the Homes before Roads lobby, had vigorously opposed the idiotic and megalomaniac road-building proposals. The change of political control in the GLC and central government in 1973/74 had brought a reprieve, but the Department of Transport hung on to the land that it had acquired on the south-east corner where the pawnbrokers epitomised the sorry state of affairs. The GLC handed their land over to Islington Council.

The GLC's Greater London Development Plan had designated the Angel as an office development area. In a bid to get something done, Islington Council decided to take a proactive role. Thus in 1976, following negotiations with the property developer Max Rayne, the remaining Georgian buildings on the west side of St John Street were pulled down, and in 1978 planning permission was granted for the Angel Centre, still set back for potential road widening.

Islington High Street in 1975. All the buildings on the far side of the road were later demolished. (Islington Planning Department)

The loss of Goose Yard and Field Place extinguished another fragment of Islington's rural past. On the north-east corner the remaining buildings of Islington High Street, which had extended considerably south of the Mall and Duncan Street, were demolished, including the surviving façade of Frank Matcham's Empire Theatre. Unlisted as it was, few people objected; most simply shrugged their shoulders and regarded it as inevitable, just as the Odeon cinema had gone from the corner of Upper Street and Florence Street in 1973, replaced by a petrol station. More attention was focused on the closure of the Underground public lavatories, which had become infested with buddleia. There were apocryphal stories of goldfish having been kept by a previous attendant in the glass tanks above the marble and brass urinals. On the west side of the High Street the auditorium of the Edwardian Angel Picture Theatre, which had closed for business in 1972, was also demolished in 1976, leaving only the slim tower and an uncertain future.

The way was now clear for some of the more unfortunate developments at the Angel. Frederick Gibberd was commissioned to design a monster block for the Royal Bank of Scotland (RBS) on the east side, but largely due to the efforts of Councillor Anne Page (wife of *New Statesman* editor Bruce Page) who lived in Duncan Terrace immediately behind the site, it was rejected. The lack of commercial interest in office development in what was regarded by the property market as a grubby and poorly served district of London (epitomised by its Monopoly-board status) meant that nothing actually got built in the 1970s. Elsom Pack Roberts' scheme for the Angel Centre and Gollins Melvin Ward's Regent's Court for the RBS would have to wait until the next decade. Meanwhile, cheap rents attracted some unlikely newcomers. In 1978 the African National Congress (ANC) set up their London headquarters in Penton Street. Around the corner at No. 57 White Lion Street, an experimental libertarian school had been established in 1972 in a solitary and scruffy Georgian house, offering an alternative education, free of compulsion or formality. It thrived and by 1978 it was taking over seventy local children.

The Odeon cinema on the corner of Upper Street and Florence Street, 1972. (English Heritage)

Chapman's hardware shop, Penton Street. (Mike Bruce)

The White Lion Free School survived, eventually under the wing of the Inner London Education Authority (ILEA) until 1990, probably the most famous of its kind in Britain.

A short way north, a bigger headache was the Royal Agricultural Hall (RAH) which occupied a huge site from Upper Street to Liverpool Road. Having been used rather unsatisfactorily by the Post Office from 1939 until 1970, it now lay empty. Initially the Council had ideas of demolition and redevelopment for housing, but in 1972 the RAH had been listed and was now seeking another use. While proposals emerged and floundered for a national ice-skating centre and a Dickens' World theme park, the fabric of this spectacular structure continued to rot. Inside the Main Hall weeds were growing through the wooden block floor, and a hard hat was essential protection from falling glass. The condition of the smaller Blue Hall Theatre and Berners Hall fronting Upper Street and the Gilbey Hall in Barford Street became so bad that demolition was deemed unavoidable. At least their clearance gave the elbow room for the eventual 1980s solution.

The Council also had ambitious plans for the Angel as a new and enlarged shopping centre, based around land at Parkfield Street and Layton Road where houses were being demolished under slum-clearance powers. The traditional stallholders of Chapel Market were seen by some as 'holding the Angel back'. What was needed was a supermarket, plenty of car parks and an inner relief road. Every other town centre in England had one, or hoped to have one, so why not Islington? Clearance of buildings such as Mandeville Houses for the Culpeper link road (now known as Tolpuddle Street) began in 1976. Once again, however, the problem was a lack of commercial interest. Even the Marks & Spencer's Angel shop was a dump, full of unsold clothes from other stores at reduced prices. The Council's property advisers, Hillier & Parker, suggested an office-led scheme, but nothing came of that either.

Back in the sanctuary of the Planning Department, while Ken Blythe's successor, Denis Browne, and his deputy, Bert Newbrook, were busy courting office developers and supermarkets, I was given humbler tasks by my boss Chris Isaac, most immediately to write the

Demolition for the Culpeper link road. (Mike Bruce)

planning brief for the Scott Estate. This was a large area of mid-Victorian housing, previously part of Lord Scott's London estate, but now owned by the Council. They had bought a job-lot of 1,000 houses for £1 million, quite a snip.

Without realising it I had arrived at Islington at a crucial time. Since coming to power in the 1971 local elections, the Labour Party was firmly in control of the Council. The Conservatives, who had ruled almost every London Borough in 1968, had been reduced to a handful of councillors. After the 1974 elections nearly all the sixty councillors were Labour, plus the ten aldermen who were elected by the ruling party. Uppermost on the political agenda was housing, and the chair of the Housing Committee was Margaret Watson (later Hodge). An equally big player, and rather more important than the Director of Housing Derek Hopkins, was Bob Trickett, Director of Development and Co-ordinator of Technical Services. He was effectively deputy to the Town Clerk or Chief Executive, Hugh Dewing, who was an intelligent but rather remote and uncharismatic figure. Trickett had a military background, but also contacts in high places, including friends in the Cabinet. While his detractors called him 'Tricky Trickett' or 'Mr Fix-it', his string-pulling, coupled with Margaret Watson's ambition and drive, secured huge funds from the post-1974 Labour government for Islington to pursue its political goals. Islington's housing budget was said to have been bigger in the mid-1970s than the GLC's, who still had major housing responsibilities across the whole of London. Trickett's small but highly competent team acquired enormous areas of Islington, including the New River, Brewers and Scott Estates.

While the 1960s craze for building high-rise blocks had dwindled, most local authorities, including Islington, were still relentlessly pursuing comprehensive redevelopment, building new low-rise estates rather than tower blocks. Huge areas of Victorian or even Georgian housing were condemned as being unfit. 'Has it got a thirty-year life?' was the usual and persistent question, and the standard and predictable answer was that tenements and long-neglected terraces with leaking roofs, outside lavatories and no hot water didn't meet that criterion, when of course a careful repair programme could have given them a 100-year life. Three early eighteenth-century houses on Islington Green went on that basis.

By 1975, Islington Council's massive rebuilding programme was in full swing, with over 150 Housing Development Areas under construction or in the pipeline. HDA1, the enormous Marquess Estate, was just being completed, right beside the office. Here, a large area of low-density Victorian villas had been acquired and replaced by very high-density, new Council housing, the idea being to produce surplus capacity so that residents could be decanted from other redevelopment areas. The architects Darbourne & Darke were the flavour of the month, the current heroes of social housing design, acclaimed for the triumph of Lillington Gardens in Pimlico. Harold Wilson did the honours at the official opening in 1975. For a few years after, when foreign delegations came to gape and grateful residents expressed their delights over their modern kitchens and bathrooms, the Marquess Estate was bathed in glory. No one foresaw that the flats roofs would leak and the labyrinthine layout of the pedestrian paths would prove impenetrable and dangerous. But postmen found it difficult to deliver letters, parts became a no-go area for the police, and no one in the office with any sense used it as a shortcut.

Islington Council was lucky to have Alf Head as its Chief Architect and Don Fletcher as his deputy. While running a huge department he was also a visionary, and skilful at standing up to Trickett and Watson when he had to. Following the outrage of the 1960s Packington Estate, where fine 1840s terraces had been demolished for a systems-built horror, Alf Head had had the sense in the early 1970s to support schemes such as Harley Sherlock's Popham Street and John Melvin's Risinghill Street, but also to refurbish listed Georgian terraces in Claremont, Myddelton and Tibberton Squares. Although the national scandal of Packington had led in part to the Parliamentary legislation for designating conservation areas, only small areas of

The east side of Islington Green in 1979, before the three old houses on the left were pulled down.
(English Heritage)

Islington had been protected and the Scott Estate was not one of them. Nevertheless, the
decision was taken that the vast majority of the 1,000 houses should be kept and refurbished,
the first large-scale, area-based rehabilitation scheme in the Borough.

My role involved frequent visits to the architects' department in Margery Street, and the
development of a good working (and drinking) relationship with the various job architects,
such as Brian Kelly, Malcolm Parker and John Ellis. Within the estate there was some
demolition, for a handful of small new-build schemes, but mainly to provide new public open
spaces and playgrounds. Rosemary Gardens was one of the seven new district parks being
created for Islington. In these clearance areas the houses were decanted and left to rot, awaiting
the demolition contractor's ball. Lampeter Street and the other sad side streets off Shepperton
Road still had their cobbles and gas lights, the empty houses left open to the elements and
the casual intruder. Through open doors and windows you could see among the abandoned
furniture and belongings how people had lived their lives.

The rehabilitation of the Scott Estate wasn't an isolated case for very long. The new Labour
government introduced Housing Action Areas (HAAs) to encourage local authorities to
take positive action in areas of multiple deprivation, and Islington Council jumped at the
opportunity, prompted by lobbying from the local Housing Action Group. Now too there
were significant technical innovations which made it easier to make old properties fit for
human habitation, particularly the introduction of injected damp-proof courses and gas
central heating, made cheaper by new boilers and North Sea gas. By 1977/78 the Council
had set up about ten HAAs and appointed a team of officers to deal with them, occupying
some spare space in our Essex Road office. In Beresford, Arthur, Offord, Alexander, Axminster,
Regina, Tabley, Hanley and Northchurch Roads, hundreds of street properties were
compulsorily purchased from negligent or impoverished private landlords. The government
then provided the funds for repairs and conversion. As part of the Local Plans team in the

Planning Department, I became involved in the concurrent improvements to the streets for which there was also funding.

The dereliction in Offord Road had largely been caused by the Ringway One motorway proposals. Nobody would have wanted to buy or invest in property faced with that threat. St Paul's Road had been similarly blighted, now also cursed with heavy lorries. With few self-interested owner-occupiers to protest, Offord Road had become the main east-west route between Liverpool Road and Caledonian Road following the Barnsbury traffic management scheme. Even streets not directly affected, such as nearby Fieldway Crescent, were semi-blighted by their proximity.

The inter-war housing estates, built by the old London County Council and Metropolitan Boroughs of Finsbury and Islington, were also a concern. The Wakelin/Halton and Northern Estates studies saved most of these from demolition, and instead recommended installing lifts, upgrading kitchens and bathrooms and other improvements. Nevertheless, several massive redevelopment schemes continued. Eric Lyons' sprawling mono-pitched red-brick estates at Delhi-Outram and Roman Way continued unabated, despite futile resistance in the siege of Lesly Street from those displaced.

The GLC had two enormous developments of their own in Holloway, the gigantic Andover and Elthorne Estates. These had been a direct result of targeted action following the government's White Paper on Housing Need, responding to the problems of Rachmanism, which had identified Tollington and North Paddington as the two worst housing areas in London. Only in Charteris Road in 1978 did residents successfully lobby the Council to overturn proposals for demolition, and only then by one vote.

The best of the 1970s new-build social housing were small scale, the last of Kenneth Pring's sensitive yellow-brick infill blocks in Barnsbury, Dry Halasz Dixon's Colebeck Mews, Darbourne and Darke's Seaforth Crescent, and the Council's own in-house schemes at Legion Close, Crown Mansions, Napier Terrace and Almorah Road. Small could be beautiful. Many of the larger schemes have not stood the test of time.

Islington, I soon discovered, was packed with industrial firms, light engineering and printers, metal workers making everything from coat hangers to stamping machines, cardboard-box manufacturers and food processors. The yard of Dove Bros builders and stonemasons still had a few pieces of granite from John Rennie's London Bridge, the majority of which had been re-erected in Arizona in 1968. The 150ft-chimney of the Ebonite factory in Tileyard Road was a local landmark. However, many of the higher-tech businesses such as Cossors electronics in Aberdeen Works had moved out to modern premises in the New Towns, leaving a residue of old-fashioned businesses in antiquated premises. Even George, who MOT'd my Morris Minor round the corner from the office at Marquess Motors, was keen to pack it in. One by one these firms closed down in the late 1970s and planners scratched their heads about what to do with the sites, which were usually zoned for employment.

Such was the lack of interest that anyone wanting to invest in commercial property was welcomed with open arms and could build pretty much what they liked, however hideous. Thus the ghastly Essex Flour and Grain Sheds at the junction of Liverpool Road/Offord Road, the red-brick bullion store on Caledonian Road/All Saints Street and the phoney Waterside Inn on the Westinghouse site at Battlebridge Basin were all rubber-stamped. In 1974 permission was given to Stuart Lipton's Sterling Land Co. for the construction of two office towers for the NatWest Bank on the north side of Pentonville Road, not only unattractive in themselves but requiring the demolition of the 1935 Lilley & Skinner shoe factory, designed by Owen Williams. Had it survived, surely today it would be listed. The first tower was finished in 1975 but the second had to be permitted as a warehouse to get round the refusal of an Office Development Permit by the Location of Offices Bureau, which was actively trying to move offices out of London. The bulky and ugly Royal Scot and Ryan hotels on King's Cross Road (now the Thistle and Travelodge) were also ushered through the planning system in the 1972 and 1976, the minor concessions being a poor pastiche Georgian façade on Percy Circus and the retention of the literary Riceyman Steps on Gwynne Place.

Only at Balfe Street in King's Cross was commercial development resisted. Here the landowners, Stock Conversion, were keen to build another Euston Tower, but the local residents, and the Thornhill Project won the day. The terraces were listed and the Council compulsorily acquired them for refurbishment.

As well as the Angel and King's Cross, the Council had four other Action Areas: Archway, Finsbury Park, Holloway's Nag's Head Shopping Centre and Highbury Corner. Lester Pritchard's team undertook surveys, wrote reports and drew up priorities, but nothing much actually happened in those areas.

To his credit, Denis Browne, who'd bought some fashionable new brown corduroy sofas for his office, was more interested in good design than Ken Blythe. Even though there was very little new-build private housing in the 1970s (Harley Sherlock's house in Alwyne Place being a notable exception), there were an increasing number of proposals to alter existing houses which had been bought by people with money to spare. With Denis' support, I introduced the idea of policies so that the hitherto whims and inconsistencies of individual officers could be better contained. Beginning originally with controls over side extensions infilling the gaps between semi-detached villas in Canonbury and then moving on to roof extensions, the concept of design-policy guidelines was born in Islington.

One of the few schemes for private housing revolved around the potential demolition of the Union Chapel, which had fallen into a sad state of disrepair and whose high Victorian architecture was not as widely appreciated as it is today. Derek Sharpe, whose architectural practice was in Compton Terrace, had the idea of putting back a copy of the original 1806 chapel with new houses on either side. Fortunately it came to nothing; a few years later the Friends of Union Chapel and a new enlightened vicar saved the day.

As a junior and inexperienced member of the Planning Department I had little contact with politicians. We knew that Barbara Castle lived in Canonbury with her husband, Ted, who was an alderman, but I was hardly aware that Jack Straw was a local councillor and Deputy Chair of the Inner London Education Authority, Donald Hoodless was Chair of Finance or that Chris Smith replaced Margaret Watson as Chair of Housing. The local paper, the *Islington Gazette*, was a rag largely devoted to smutty crime reports or bonnie baby competitions and not the place to glean inside information. There were allegations of gerrymandering when it was claimed that newly acquired Council street properties in Barnsbury were being allocated to short-life user groups (SLUGS) with good socialist credentials and voting intentions. The dead-heat election in 1978 in Clerkenwell when the Council leader, Gerry Southgate, had to draw straws with the Tory Don Bromfield (and won) also caused a stir.

I had little interaction even with those few councillors and aldermen who were interested in planning: Morris Perry, George Taylor, Jeffrey Fairweather and David Hyams. My main contact was with the dreaded Bill and Audrey Baylis on the Scott Estate Sub-Committee. Bill was old-guard Labour, an intimidating disciplinarian, highly conservative and generally negative in outlook. 'I don't mind when officers recommend refusal,' he would say, 'it's when they recommend approval that I get worried'.

As for the MPs, George Cunningham for Islington South and Michael O'Halloran for Islington North, I never met either of them. Some said that O'Halloran would do anything for you if you were Irish, and that he could do no wrong. In the end both were to jump ship to the Social Democratic Party, and were voted out of office to be replaced by Chris Smith and Jeremy Corbyn. At some stage in the late 1970s, the aldermen also disappeared when that anachronistic system was abolished.

Life in the Planning Department was relaxed. Among a generally genial bunch there were a few strong or awkward characters, such as chief admin officer, Ron Langton, and his assistant, Alan Pickett, who reckoned they really kept the place ship-shape, and Tony Dyer who was in charge of rushing through all the planning applications for the Council's own developments. He had the unnerving habit of answering the phone, with his West Country accent, 'Dyer 'ere'.

Lily was on the switchboard and front desk, knew all the gossip, but still found time to knit prodigiously. In the office everything was written by hand and sent, if necessary, to the typing pool, to be done on the latest electric machines in triplicate, with white and yellow carbon copies. May Moore took dictation in Pitman shorthand, and a few techno-wizards used the unreliable Dictaphone. There was a huge and cumbersome photocopier, but no fax. The Computer Department of the Council was still in its infancy in premises opposite the Town Hall in Upper Street, and spent most of its resources grappling with financial figures, although the land use survey team in the Planning Department used punch-cards and could obtain bulky paper printouts.

The department was quite militantly unionised, not exactly a NALGO closed shop, but infinitely more so than suburban Harrow. There I had missed out on the eight-week strike in 1973/74 (on full pay) over London weighting, when the union activist Will Fancy had achieved huge solidarity in inner London. There were shorter strikes in 1978 and 1979, but the union coffers by then were running low.

Social life in the office involved lengthy sessions in the local pubs, usually the nearby Marquess Tavern in Canonbury Street, and often on Fridays a stroll or bike ride further afield to the Island Queen, the Empress of Russia or the Rising Sun in Brooksby Street. In warm, sunny weather the garden of the Canonbury Tavern was the winner. Very little work was done on Friday afternoons. Unlike Harrow, where we'd had to wear jackets and ties, dress code in the office was non-existent, and lots of people smoked cigarettes, pipes, even cigars. To say that it was not a target-driven culture was an understatement. The flexi-time system seemed to be as flexible as you wanted to make it.

There were active football and cricket teams, with a departmental kitbag. The new all-weather artificial football pitches at Market Road installed in 1976 were a tremendous boon, and the usual venue for our soccer matches – including our greatest victory, 11-1 against the Parks Department. Finding a cricket ground wasn't so easy in Islington, hence the trek out to Hackney Marshes.

Adjoining the rear part of our office was Daneman's piano factory in Northampton Street. They employed a number of blind piano tuners and technicians, who every morning and late afternoon would shuffle along the pavement, white sticks tapping, between the bus stops and the factory entrance. Daneman's was not at the top end of piano manufacture, mainly churning out modern uprights for schools, and doomed to closure when they were undercut by Japanese and Korean competition, but on a couple of occasions they were kind enough to loan us an instrument for our office Christmas party. By good fortune there was a connecting opening with sliding doors on rollers between their factory and our rear first floor, where a large clear space was used for filing, and parties. Drunken and full-throated sing-songs led by my colleagues Linda, Len, Peter and Mike, with me busking on the keyboard, were tempered only by minor anxiety that too much beer might get poured into the mechanism.

✑ CLERKENWELL ✑

When I started working in Islington in 1975, the amalgamation of the old Boroughs of Finsbury and Islington into the new London Borough of Islington was only ten years old. While the merger had gone more smoothly than in some of the larger Boroughs where there was less political unity, there were still underlying currents of discontent. Finsbury had been comparatively rich, with a higher rate income and a smaller population than old Islington. It had also been a far more progressive local authority both before and after the war, with a very active Housing Committee and many more high-rise and high-density estates to show for it. Some of these, such as Finsbury Estate, had been completed only recently and still had a fresh crispness. Others such as the Triangle and the St Luke's Estate were still under construction. So too were the new buildings for the City University along Spencer Street, where only half the houses in Northampton Square had escaped demolition.

There was a different and modern feel to Finsbury, which Georgian and Victorian Islington lacked. Several of the post-war primary schools, such as Prior Weston, were held in such high esteem that normal catchment areas were stretched for those parents who could pull strings (Paul McCartney and David Owen among them). The clean lines of Lubetkin's Finsbury Health Centre in Pine Street contrasted with the grubby brick of Royal Free Hospital in Liverpool Road and the Royal Northern in Holloway Road, which offered Dickensian prospects of medical provision.

Despite the unification there had been no rationalisation of Council office accommodation, which was scattered around numerous different sites. The Town Clerk, solicitors and committee rooms were in Islington Town Hall in Upper Street, while the Registrar of Births, Marriages and Deaths was in old Finsbury Town Hall in Rosebery Avenue. The Coordinator of Technical Services and the Housing Action Area team shared the Planning Department offices while the main Housing Department was in another former factory at No. 292 Essex Road. The Valuers rented a house in Compton Terrace before moving down to Old Street, the Parks Department was on the corner of Holloway Road and Camden Road, Social Services were in the old

The entrance to Clerkenwell Close from Clerkenwell Green, 1979. (English Heritage)

Edwards Factory in Islington Park Street and the local District Surveyor's office, still then part of the GLC, was in Club Union House at Highbury Corner.

The Borough Engineers' Department was responsible for all highways, traffic and transport planning matters, except for the main trunk roads controlled by central government. My attempts to promote various road closures for the Scott Estate thus took me to their offices in Clerkenwell Road, a fine, late Victorian red-brick building originally occupied by the Holborn Board of Guardians. The Borough Engineer was Bob Woodhead, a blunt and brusque Yorkshireman with little time for planners and traffic management. 'Woodhead in name and Woodhead in nature' was our mischievous parody, though I'm sure he did an excellent job on maintaining the carriageways. A Borough-wide campaign was in full swing, removing the 'hazardous' York stone from the pavements and laying regular concrete slabs instead.

The engineers used a vacant and levelled bomb-site on the north side of Clerkenwell Green next to the Marx Memorial Library as their staff car park. This was one of a number of empty sites in Clerkenwell which the London County Council had earmarked years previosuly for future public open space. It was probably a throwback to the idealistic pre-war Finsbury Plan, when the whole area was intended to be redeveloped with new blocks of flats, schools and health centres in an idyllic Corbusian setting of trees and grass.

Meanwhile, the population figures which justified the large amount of parkland were questionable, particularly as many of the nineteenth-century tenements where most people had lived were being flattened. First to go was Corporation Buildings, replaced in 1975 by Elsom Pack Roberts' unattractive offices for the *Guardian* newspaper, followed in 1976 by Victoria Dwellings on the corner with Clerkenwell Road and Farringdon Road Buildings opposite the Eagle public house. The biggest loss was Northampton Buildings, which had once housed 4,000 people, occupying a complete street block south of Skinner Street. Coldbath Buildings near the fire station on Rosebery Avenue was temporarily spared, optimistically renamed Springfield Court, and offered to a short-life housing co-op.

The Topham/Warner site, behind the Eagle pub, still had a few post-war pre-fabs in 1975, but the last of these were removed and the empty land given to National Car Parks, who also took over all the other cleared sites, cunningly negotiated with the Borough Valuer. That in itself was a recipe for inaction. My involvement and task was to change the zoning of these sites from open space, and to persuade the GLC officers in their County Hall ivory tower (and the car drivers in the Borough Engineers) to agree. Although nothing actually got built in the economic doldrums of the 1970s on these sites, at least it paved the way for something to happen in the 1980s.

Most of Clerkenwell Close was similarly blighted, all the way down to Clerkenwell Green, leaving only the historic church unscathed in a sea of dereliction. There were even idiotic GLC plans to expand the Victorian Hugh Myddelton Primary and Secondary Schools, despite both having ceased to be schools. Many of the old properties had fallen into a lamentable state. Even when the blight was lifted some owners proved difficult to deal with, most notably the orthodox-Jewish Grussgott brothers and the Joshua Trust, who owned the Weavers Cottages and ran a business nearby in Hatton Garden. Compulsory purchase powers eventually sorted this out, rationalised the boundaries of the churchyard park, repaired the cottages and Georgian houses and provided a site for new social and sheltered housing. One of their other sites was in Herbal Hill, where the remnants of St Andrew's Workhouse (featured in *Oliver Twist*) had been pulled down in the early 1970s.

Another casualty was the Tarbox factory in St James's Walk, one of hundreds of small businesses struggling to make a living in Clerkenwell. As in Islington, further north many of the large-scale industries were closing down or moving out, leaving the minnows behind to fend for themselves. Clerkenwell had been famous for its brewing and distilling, but the 1970s saw their demise. The sprawling Cannon Brewery in St John Street had been taken over by Allied Domecq, who closed down the brewing function in 1977, leaving only offices and empty buildings. In 1979 I worked on the first planning brief for the site. Similarly, the magnificent 250-year-old Whitbread Brewery in Chiswell Street stopped making beer in 1976, although they did maintain a distribution depot and the stabling for their dray horses in Garrett Street. The vacuum was eventually filled by converting the old Porter Tun Room and Sugar Room into a banqueting hall and conference facilities, skilfully carried out in 1977 by Wolff Olins and Roderick Gradidge. North of Whitbread Street, less happily, most of the unlisted brewery buildings were demolished in 1978-79 and replaced by the turgid brown brick of Cherry Tree Walk facing Whitecross Street, designed by Saillard Fuller & Partners.

The distilleries fared no better. Booths Gin had occupied a series of buildings on Clerkenwell Road and Turnmill Street including the tall 1956 distillery on the corner with Britton Street, one of the last industrial structures of any architectural merit to be built in Clerkenwell. The giant copper stills could be seen from the street through the long multi-paned windows. Manufacture stopped in 1974, and as part of an office redevelopment designed by Yorke Rosenberg Mardall the fine Edwardian frontage on Turnmill Street was carefully dismantled and re-erected in 1977 as a façade to Britton Street, with sleek and elegant modern offices behind. Nicholson's Gin had closed in 1970 and their magnificent Georgian distillery fronting St John Street, with a double layer of vaulted basements for bonded warehousing, was now being used, less attractively, by Woodhouse Hume for meat processing. By the end of the decade only Gordon's distillery in Moreland Street was still operating.

Next to Nicolson's, on the corner of Sekforde Street, the vacant Myerson's Ironworks proved difficult to develop, and the closure of Smith's non-ferrous metals in St John's Square left a row of empty, run-down Georgian houses.

Despite this there were still hundreds of manufacturing businesses in Clerkenwell, many associated with the print trade, conveniently close to Fleet Street, or the rag trade supplying the West End, and jewellers providing components or specialist trades for Hatton Garden. Some operated in extraordinary conditions, such as the Albion Wire Works, which had hot metal presses thundering away in the panelled rooms of a 1720s house in Britton Street, or the Uniform Clothing Co., which made the finest military-dress tunics and braids in a badly-lit labyrinth on Clerkenwell Green.

Clerkenwell's greatest tradition was watches and clocks, and dozens of these workshops, makers, repairers, wholesalers and retailers survived in the 1970s. Mr Gafan operated from a shop on Clerkenwell Road barely big enough to turn round in, while Rowley and Parkes' workshop in Briset Street was approached up a steep flight of rickety wooden stairs, the solid work bench cluttered with a thousand cogs, an ordered jumble of dismantled timepieces. As Dan Parkes warmed his hands in front of the open fire, nothing here seemed to have changed for centuries.

There were glum forecasts about the future of industry in the inner city. The Scholl's shoe factory in St John Street was threatened with closure, while the depletion of the local workforce persuaded many of the clothing firms to move out to the Cypriot areas of Finsbury Park and Kentish Town.

But not all was gloom and doom. Newcomers to the area included the ecclesiastical silversmith Michael Murray and the Australian goldsmith Stuart Devlin in St John Street, who by 1978 was employing fifty apprentices making hand-raised goblets, bracelets, cutlery and ornaments. In 1976 a group of enterprising young entrepreneurs, led by Mike Franks and Neil Jackson, took a five-year lease from the GLC on the redundant LCC Supplies warehouse in Clerkenwell Close. Urban Small Space Ltd offered small, fully serviced workshops and cheap

Nos 45-49 Clerkenwell Close, 1975. (English Heritage)

Farringdon Road Book Market. (Theo Bergström)

weekly rents, which proved incredibly attractive to start-up businesses. Clerkenwell Workshops was born, and was soon full to overflowing with 300 craftsmen.

The government's 1978 Inner Urban Areas Act offered new hope with loans and grants for areas of run-down industrial buildings, aiming to stabilise and regenerate the economic life of older commercial areas. This stirred the Council into action. Bob Trickett, apparently on friendly terms with Denis Healey, secured Treasury funds to invest in two buildings on Clerkenwell Road, originally acquired for road widening but transferred to Islington by the GLC. Under the aegis of the newly formed Clerkenwell Green Association, Pennybank Chambers and Cornwell House were converted in 1978/79 into craft workshops, where their cellular brick structure proved ideal. The renaissance had begun.

Under the same legislation Clerkenwell, together with Vale Royal off York Way and Whitecross Street, was designated as an Industrial Improvement Area. I was part of the delegation which trooped off to the ghastly Department of Environment blocks in Marsham Street to put our case to John Sinkiewicz, happily successfully. Thus it was that I came to sit beside Dan Parkes on his apprentice's stool as he regaled me about 'lost' Clerkenwell while I offered him a grant to repair the roof of his garret in Briset Street.

I soon discovered that Clerkenwell had its 'characters': Mrs Lloyd in her time-warp dairy in Amwell Street, Cyril Oliver who scraped a living from his auto-spares shop at No. 6 Clerkenwell Close, and Mr Jeffery who ran the second-hand book market on Farringdon Road. This was the rump of what had once been a thriving market north of Holborn Viaduct which had sold all manner of non-perishable goods. Now there were just half-a-dozen trestle tables, piled with books, maps and prints. It was a Mecca for book dealers and tatterdemalion bargain hunters who might find a first edition hidden amongst the faded spines. Nobody quite knew where Mr Jeffery got his books from, but every weekday morning he would take them by trolley from his store opposite Mr Oliver to the Farringdon Road kerbside, just south of the junction with Clerkenwell Road, and after lunch, take them back again. He was a one-man band and when he went, so did the market.

Exmouth Market also seemed to be in terminal decline, with the migration of so many local residents and the loss of lunchtime trade. Half the shops were closed, the upper floors mainly empty, and there were rumours of redevelopment. Whitecross Street had a more prosperous midday market, supported by office workers from Chiswell Street and Finsbury Square as well as local residents, but the side streets were beset with the problems of declining industries, particularly the dwindling Shoreditch furniture trade. The ruins of St Luke's Church on Old Street didn't help the image of the area. To most passers-by this looked like yet another bomb-site, and I was shocked to find out later that the Diocese had made the church redundant and removed the roof in 1958. Some of the internal fittings were moved to St Giles' Cripplegate. In 1975, as Islington's gesture towards European Architectural Heritage Year, a new conservation area was designated around the church and derelict churchyard, which didn't achieve much at the time but no doubt improved its long-term prospects.

In Clerkenwell there were rumblings of potential development on some larger sites. In 1978 Reuters news agency moved into and adapted the fortress-like brown-brick monster in Great Sutton Street, designed by Ronald Trebilcock. In December 1979 I got to meet Richard Seifert, or the Colonel as he was known, a sobriquet which had followed him from his Army days in Burma. Here was the architect who had done more than any other to change the face of 1970s London. His firm, then the largest in London, had been hired to look at two sites, one at the bottom end of St John Street and the other the derelict Farringdon Goods Depot on Farringdon Road and Cowcross Street, and the dapper little man came to our humble office in Essex Road to explain his ideas. During the meeting his chauffeur kept the Rolls Royce ticking over outside in Canonbury Street and the larger of his two well-built companions hovered by the door. It was an unlikely place for an assassination, and I'm sure I was more afraid of him than he of me. Besides, Seifert had designed one of his better buildings in Islington, the Sobell Centre, and Sue Seifert was to become one of Islington's finest head teachers.

In the end Roger Zogolovitch developed the St John Street site and the hulk of the goods depot was left to rot for another ten years. I tried to get it listed, but Mike Gilman, who was our regular contact at the GLC Historic Buildings Division, wasn't interested.

Clerkenwell proved to be endlessly fascinating, both above and below ground. I had my first introduction to archaeology with the excavation of the medieval walls of St Mary's Nunnery at Clerkenwell Close in 1976. Guided by the friendly enthusiasm of Pamela Willis and Stella Dyer at St John's Gate, I enjoyed my first visit to the astonishing crypt below St John's Church. The Master and Bursar showed me the hidden delights of the Charterhouse, the monks' cells and the lay brothers' hatch.

What struck me as odd was that so few people actually lived south of the Clerkenwell Road, just a handful of publicans and caretakers above their daytime premises. My colleagues in the Planning Department spent their time agonising over whether redundant industrial or warehouse premises could change their use to offices (all still at that time in separate Use Classes). When I suggested that private residential use might be considered and promoted, even the idea of mixed use with flats on upper floors and commercial use below, everybody thought I was mad, not only the planners but developers and estate agents too. Who in their right mind would want to live in a dump like Clerkenwell? That, I'm afraid, would have to wait for another decade.

∾ VENTURING SOUTH OF THE RIVER ∾

Before coming to live in London my knowledge of south of the river was at best patchy. Large areas were the equivalent of 'here be dragons' on medieval maps. While still a student in Cambridge I'd been to a party at Buxton Orr's elegant lower-ground flat in the Paragon Blackheath, and I knew the immediate environs of Tulse Hill where my then girlfriend shared a flat. We'd walked a couple of times in Brockwell Park and been to a seedy cinema on Streatham High Road to see *A Clockwork Orange*. I knew a tiny part of Battersea from my post-graduate course at the Polytechnic, and I knew, all too well, everything you could see from the railway viaducts through Bromley South and into Victoria Station, a vision of suburban rear gardens, the higgledy-piggledy backs of grimy Victorian terraces, rows of chimney pots, glimpses into factory yards and wide expanses of overgrown railway sidings.

In April 1974, one of the inmates in the house in Hendon had moved to Norbury. Dave was a gregarious and sociable chap, and had got into conversation, by chance, with an elderly man who was back in London for the first time for forty years. He had bought a new house in the 1930s, but emigrated soon after to Australia, taking the keys of the house with him. Having been back in London for a few weeks he'd decided he didn't like it and was about to return to the outback. He gave Dave the keys to the house. On several occasions the rest of us in Hendon piled into my Morris Minor and we made the long trip south. The house was an unremarkable semi from the outside, but inside a 1930s time-warp.

We drank in the magnificent Pied Bull pub on Streatham High Road, probably once a coaching inn on the road to Brighton, but now a huge Young's hostelry with a selection of rooms for different clientele, even a smart saloon with waitress service. Next door was Cow's India Rubber Works and a disused textile mill with a cupola, apparently designed to attract Spitalfields silk weavers, which many years later was to become a Sainsbury's supermarket. It was an even longer trip home to Hendon, but much handier for Dave who was studying at the Brixton School of Building.

Brixton Market arcades. (Theo Bergström)

Brixton Market was a great discovery, and after moving to the Kensington flat it was within striking range by bike, augmented by new panniers to carry our prizes home. This was a hugely different affair to the East End Sunday markets at Club Row or Petticoat Lane, or the work-a-day stalls of Chapel Market and Whitecross Street in Islington. Brixton offered an extraordinary range and variety of products, most of which I'd never seen or heard of before, and as the centre of South London's West Indian community it reflected the full gamut of Caribbean life. Even the street names, Electric Avenue and Atlantic Road, had an exciting flavour.

The oldest section of the market was Electric Avenue, with the longest established traders, although most of these had changed with the times to meet their customers' requirements. Between Atlantic Road and Coldharbour Lane the market sprawled into arcades and alleys beneath and either side of the railway viaducts. The streets throbbed with animated chatter and laughter, women bartering and haggling with the stallholders for their food. Everywhere the music of Bob Marley pounded out from the boom boxes and prototype ghetto blasters in the record shops. The choice of tropical fruit and vegetables was astonishing: yams, sweet potatoes, bread fruit, cho-cho, cassava, green bananas, coconuts and mangos. The butchers' slabs were piled with pink pigs' tails and trotters, cows' feet and yellow sides of beef. The grocers sold tinned ackee and salt fish, egusi seeds, kola nuts, soursubs and patties. Strangest were the fishmongers who offered the weird and wonderful contents of the Caribbean Sea: red mullet, flying fish, shark, tuna and goat fish, and many other intimidating specimens besides. You probably needed to be West Indian to know what to do with them.

Brixton seemed to be the best possible reason for ever wanting to live in South London. The market buzzed with gaiety and good humour. In the summer of 1976, everyone was talking cricket. Perhaps the dereliction of the Victorian canopies in Electric Avenue, where rainwater cascaded onto the pavements rather than protecting the shoppers, was symptomatic of the lack of civic investment into the area which, together with heavy-handed policing, would fuel discontent. As a naïve and occasional casual visitor I could not have predicted the riots and Scarman report. Nor did I know that there were still idiotic plans to redevelop Central Brixton, including the market, with towers and slab blocks. Ted Hollamby's brutal 1970 Recreation Centre and multi-storey car park in Station Road were no doubt part of the grand plan, not abandoned until 1979.

I had finished my part-time planning course at the Polytechnic of the South Bank before it moved from Battersea into new purpose-built premises in Wandsworth Road and London Road, Southwark, in 1976. Neither of these turned out to be inspiring buildings, being inward-looking and presenting desolate frontages to the street. I therefore didn't get to know the Elephant and Castle as I might otherwise have done, or East Street Market off Walworth Road, which rivalled Brixton for size if not Caribbean jollity, and had the usual surliness of cockney London.

Gordon, Janie and Robin, clarinet, oboe and horn-playing friends from several orchestras, were living above a dental practice in Clapham, a rather grand, white stuccoed villa at No. 1 South Side on the corner with Crescent Grove. We sometimes rehearsed wind quintets in the living room of their flat before adjourning to the Olde Windmill on the Common or the more basic Prince of Wales in Clapham Old Town. Robin was working as an engineer on the construction of the Thames Barrier, which had begun in 1974. Geoff and I even cycled one fine spring day to see it, a long slog through Charlton and Woolwich.

I was most intrigued by those parts of the South Bank which were closest to the river and where many changes were underway or proposed. Sea Containers House was already an unpleasant blot on the Thames-side landscape, part of Richard Seifert's 1970 King's Reach development, providing a hotel and offices, and the strange multi-levelled Doggett's pub beside

Bankside Power Station still generating electricity, with demolition in the foreground near Southwark Bridge. (Mike Bruce)

Blackfriars Bridge. The Edger Estate on the other side of Blackfriars Bridge, begun in 1974, was better, and the oddly marooned single-storey Founders Arms pub sat in front of it near the Bankside Power Station. Nobody at the time could have imagined the Tate Modern. Even though the Shakespeare Globe Trust had been set up in 1970, an actual theatre was still just a pipedream in the mind of Sam Wanamaker. Although the Founders Arms served Young's beers and had a good view of the City across the water, we preferred the Prince William Henry on Blackfriars Road, equally modern but where the 'musos' congregated after South Bank concerts. Some, with a train to catch from Waterloo, went to the Hole in the Wall in one of the railway arches near the station, but there was always the risk of the carriages rumbling overhead shaking brick dust into your beer.

I already knew the Festival Hall from National Youth Orchestra concerts but the Hayward Gallery, Queen Elizabeth Hall and Purcell Room were still new, the external concrete as yet unstained and unstreaked by dirty rainwater and the undercroft only just discovered in the latest craze of skateboarding. The great anticipation and common talking point was the National Theatre, which had been under construction on the east side of Waterloo Bridge since the adoption of Denys Lasdun's final design in 1967. Now, in 1976, it was finally finished and opened with well-deserved pomp. Criticism of the architecture was muted at the time, perhaps out of relief for its completion. There was no hint of the vitriol which would come later with Prince Charles' put-down ('a clever way of building a nuclear power station in the middle of London without anyone objecting').

More attention was placed, quite rightly, on what was going on inside this new factory of theatre; Noel Coward's *Blithe Spirit*, Alan Ayckbourn's *Bedroom Farce* and a new stage adaptation of Fiona Thompson's *Lark Rise*. Peter Hall's production of *Volpone* and John Schlessinger's *Julius Caesar* were magnificent. Tom Stoppard was at his zenith, with *Jumpers* and *Every Good Boy*

Deserves Favour, while David Hare's *Plenty*, Pinter's *Betrayal* and Peter Shaffer's *Amadeus* were all new productions first seen at the National. Paul Scofield and Simon Callow were the stars in the shadow of Olivier and Gielgud.

Mike from the Planning Department office in Islington lived within a stone's throw of the National, in one of the quaint but run-down two-storey terraced streets which had escaped bombing and slum clearance. According to some sources, the population of this district had declined from 50,000 in 1901 to only 4,000 in 1971. His house in Roupell Street was the only one to enjoy a flat roof and sun deck, and this was much admired and enjoyed on various gastronomic office outings. Through Mike I learnt about Coin Street, one of several large cleared sites nearby which were owned partly by the GLC and partly by property developers. When proposals emerged in 1977 to build more than 1 million sq. ft of offices and what promised to be Europe's highest hotel, the Coin Street Action Group was set up to combat the plans. It was a classic case of two opposite camps: the local community led by Iain Tuckett, who wanted low-rise social housing, workshops, leisure facilities and a riverside park, versus the 'evil' office developer with Richard Rogers in tow as architect. To begin with the GLC were in cahoots with the developer; only in 1981 did they change camps and back the community scheme.

The so-called 'Green Giant' was an even more celebrated threat, a site on the south side of Vauxhall Bridge which had lain empty for most of the 1970s. In 1979 the property magnate Keith Wickenden proposed a new 500ft-tower to house the Tate's collection of modern art, as well as an awful lot of offices and flats. Bankside would have had a different future had that gone ahead.

Further east along the riverside were extraordinary areas of abandoned wharves and warehouses, and the occasional delightful discovery such as the remarkably squalid Becky's Dive Bar on Southwark Street under the old Hop Exchange. Becky's two-room basement bar was approached down a treacherously steep staircase and dear old Becky herself served the beer, usually Ruddles County and Old Peculier, tapped straight from the wood, 44p a pint in 1979. The stench in the gents made it no place to linger. It might as well have discharged straight into the river.

The barrow boy pubs of Borough Market were rough. The old George Inn off Southwark High Street was more respectable, and not yet inundated with tourists. In June 1979 Southwark became something of a Mecca for CAMRA fans when David Bruce opened the first microbrewery and brew pub in England at the Goose and Firkin in Borough Road, a formula so successful that it was soon followed by the Frog, the Fox, the Flounder, the Pheasant and many more elsewhere in London.

Meanwhile, the old Barclay & Perkins' Anchor Brewery on Southwark Bridge Road had been taken over and closed down by Courage and in 1976 was picturesquely derelict, eventually demolished in 1981 leaving only the ancient Anchor Inn beside the river. Next to Tower Bridge the old Horsleydown Brewery was still being operated by Courage, but soon to be closed and replaced by a new keg factory beside the M4 at Reading. Hay's Wharf, Butler's Wharf and New Concordia Wharf were vacant. The canyon-like warehouses and cock-eyed wrought-iron bridges across the tidal inlet at Shad Thames and St Saviour's Dock were probably the most dramatic industrial survivors of the Blitz. There was a sense of hiatus, waiting for something to happen. It eventually did, starting in 1977 with T.P. Bennett's Southwark Towers, then Minerva House in 1979 by Twigg, Brown & Partners who would eventually transform Hay's Wharf into Hay's Galleria.

There were plans for a Thames-side path but they were far from realised. When we finally reached Rotherhithe on our bikes and discovered the welcome rewards of the Mayflower and Angel taverns, it had involved endlessly frustrating detours around empty sites cordoned off with corrugated iron or buildings where there was no way past. Beyond us lay the vast and

Derelict docks on the South Bank. (Mike Bruce)

Greenwich Park looking north towards the docks. (Theo Bergström)

impenetrable wasteland of Surrey Docks, almost encircled by Rotherhithe Street. The Costa del Icon, as Graham Morrison was later to call the spoliation of the south bank of the river downstream from Wandsworth had yet to take shape.

The biggest adventure south of the river occurred in Greenwich. Graham, who had been a contemporary, friend and squash opponent at college in Cambridge, was by now working in Martin Richardson's architectural practice in London (designing housing in Milton Keynes) and living in a flat in Defoe House in the Barbican. We continued to play squash in London and compare notes about planning and architecture.

We also shared an idealistic view about the potential benefits of communal living. The opportunity arose in 1975 when the RAF Children's School in Greenwich closed and its premises came onto the market the following year. This private prep school had occupied Vanbrugh Castle, the Grade I listed mansion built by Sir John Vanbrugh for himself in 1718. Together with the Victorian house immediately around the corner on Westcombe Park Road, the whole lot was for sale at £100,000. Armed with the agent's details Graham and I went to see it and marvelled at its position overlooking Greenwich Park and with views at the rear across the river to the Isle of Dogs. The house itself was a fantasy of towers and turrets, extravagant chimneys, spiral staircases and crenellated parapets. In two acres of grounds there were tennis courts, a small copse of trees and a detached 1930s theatre. Even though the former dormitories, classrooms and lavatory blocks were riddled with bulky radiators and institutional pipe work, our imaginations were fired. Graham sketched out how the different wings could be divided into separate self-contained units, but most exciting was the vision of a communal library, music room, and theatre.

The asking price was way beyond our combined resources and we needed a like-minded consortium. Several friends who were already on the property ladder and potentially had houses or flats to sell were interested, even my colleague Geoff Gribble in the Islington office who lived in nearby Coleraine Road. For a few weeks we lived in hope, but it was not to be. Vanbrugh Castle was eventually sold to a group of stockbrokers who created a series of maisonettes in 1979.

How different life might have been had we, by some stroke of fortune, raised the money. Had I moved to Greenwich I doubt that I would have tolerated for very long a gruesome commute to Islington through the Blackwall tunnel and would have tried to find a job nearer. I might even have given up local government planning and looked to make Vanbrugh Castle a part of Greenwich's cultural life. Whenever I subsequently went to Greenwich, to play in St Alfege's Church and drink in the Mitre afterwards, there was always a feeling of 'what might have been'.

ꕔ FOUR MEN ON A BANK ꕔ

Possibly inspired by *Three Men in a Boat* and fuelled by beer in the Builders' Arms in Kensington, we had the idea in early 1976 of walking along the River Thames from London to Oxford. The plan was to camp on the way and carry our stuff in backpacks. Having perused the OS maps we reckoned that it was about 120 miles following the meandering course of the river, as opposed to only about fifty miles by road, and somewhat ambitiously gave ourselves six days to complete it. Easter was late in April that year, from the 16th to the 19th, and seemed ideal.

Chris and I set off from the south side of Putney Bridge mid-morning on the Wednesday before Easter, striding with some enthusiasm along the towpath alongside the course of the Boat Race, past Watney's Stag Brewery at Mortlake, Kew Gardens and Old Deer Park. After some lubrication in Richmond and again in Kingston, we crossed to the north bank after dusk and followed the seemingly unending wall of Hampton Court Park to reach the palace.

Outside the Cross Guns public house, Avoncliff, near the end of the Kennet-Avon Canal, October 1976. (Roger Forshaw)

With nowhere obvious to camp we staggered into the Mitre on Hampton Court Green to revive our no-longer sprightly legs and fill our empty stomachs. When we emerged after closing time at 10.45 p.m., it was pouring with rain. As we scurried across Hampton Bridge and turned right onto the riverbank, we were desperate to find somewhere to camp. Soon we were away from the glare of the streetlights and within a few minutes I spied a hole in the hedge beside the path which led onto a field, and there with great haste we pitched our tent. It was flat and even, and easy to push in the pegs. We were awoken from our slumbers at 6.00 a.m. by the revving of an engine and the oaths of a man. We had erected our tent right in the middle of the central square of a cricket ground and the groundsman had come to prepare the pitch. He was not amused and we left in a hurry.

From there on we were blessed with good weather. It was just as well we made an early start on the Thursday because the walk to Windsor and Eton was long and gruelling, much of it on tarmac or unforgiving cinder and clinker track, and passed the ribbon development of West Molesey, Sunbury and Shepperton, a thousand bungalows and boat houses, filter beds and playing fields. We lunched in Walton-on-Thames and again in Chertsey and arrived at the pre-agreed pub, the Waterman's Arms in Eton High Street, as the sun was setting. There we met up with Tim and Geoff, who'd been working in London and caught the train. On our way to the pub we'd skirted a meadow by the river where a metal notice read 'Property of Eton College. No Camping'. While we were surveying the scene, a little man in a bowler hat, rather like a Cambridge college porter, appeared and repeated rather prosaically the content of the notice, no doubt having seen our brightly coloured backpacks from afar. After dark we crossed the meadow, climbed over the stile and pitched our two tents on a farmer's field nearer to the bypass bridge.

The next four days were as good as a riverside walk could get, given that there was as yet no official riverside path. The Dew Drop in Honey Lane, Hurley, and a sunny lunchtime sitting out on the terrace of the Angel on the Bridge at Henley were highlights, Chris sating his appetite for scotch eggs and all of us delirious on Brakspear's Special. We camped beside the river near Marlow and up in the woods north of Reading, where we found a rustic Gales Ales pub which still had bottled Prize Old Ale with corked stoppers. On a hot Saturday afternoon, Tim's transistor radio was glued to his ear as he listened to QPR losing 3-2 to Norwich and Liverpool beating Stoke 5-3, with much gnashing of teeth.

Occasionally we had to trespass to keep close to the river, and a few outraged owners took exception to the cut of our jibs. Most of the ferries marked on the maps no longer functioned, and once we were helped across by a motorboat. After negotiating the Goring 'gap' we spent the night of Easter Sunday at Wallingford, enjoying the comforts of the Coachmakers Arms and an idyllic campsite on the water meadows. The next morning, as the sun burnt the dew off the grass, we made a detour to admire the glorious view of Didcot Power Station from the heights and ramparts of Wittenham Clumps.

We never made it to Oxford. On reaching Clifton Hampden we found the Plough Inn up the hill and there, sitting in the orchard under the apple blossom, we decided that drinking the mellow Ushers' beer was a better way to spend the Bank Holiday afternoon than plodding on to Abingdon. Down the road, beyond the UK Atomic Energy Research Centre, we found Culham Railway Station and a train back to London. Thus ended the first beer walk.

It was followed by others. The Kennet-Avon Canal from Reading to Bath in October 1976 was an obvious sequel to the Thames, and particularly good because the canal was still derelict, devoid of people and boats. The deserted flight of locks at Devizes and the isolated Barge pub at Honey Street were unexpected delights. My brother, who'd moved to Bath, joined us for some light refreshment in the Cross Guns pub at Avoncliff. The Llangollen Canal, Offa's Dyke, the Dorset coast, the South Downs Way, Hadrian's Wall and the Ridgeway were all conquered with the same winning recipe, about two-and-a-half miles walked for every pint drunk. The four of us (or three after Geoff had left for Belgium) always camped rough, usually in a tent but once or twice in a railway station waiting room, a pig sty or under a bridge.

It was a good way to get to know England, through the soles of one's feet, and London always felt a better place on my return than when I'd left it.

✎ SMITHFIELD ✎

Early in 1976 I was 'volunteered' in the office at Islington to attend a meeting with planning officers from the City Corporation. The subject was Smithfield, and the possibility of undertaking a joint cross-boundary study to provide planning guidance for what seemed an uncertain future.

The Greater London Development Plan had suggested that all of the great wholesale markets should be located out of central London, stating that 'the GLC is not satisfied that the redevelopment of London's wholesale markets on their traditional sites will result in an efficient or profitable pattern of distribution'. The City Corporation owned and controlled the Spitalfields Fruit and Veg Market, Billingsgate Fish Market beside the Thames near London Bridge, the Leadenhall Game and Provisions Market in the heart of the City, and largest of all, the huge Smithfield Meat Market, right on the northern edge of their boundary with Islington. The apparently successful move of Covent Garden Market to Nine Elms had set minds thinking within the various Corporation committees.

The Smithfield Joint Study and Plan was a novel idea, two local authorities which were poles apart politically and ideologically deciding to work together over a common problem. While

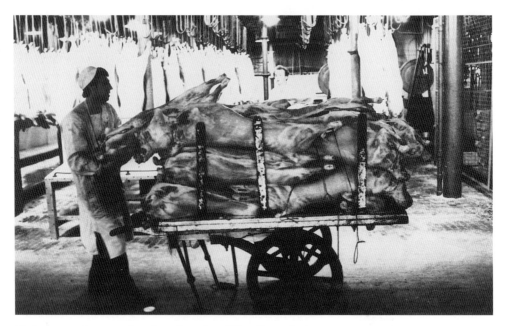

Pitchers at work among the spit-and-sawdust. (Theo Bergström)

the market lay within the City, many of the workforce lived locally in Islington, and most of the associated meat trade industries and offices also occupied premises on the Islington side of the border. From a professional point of view it was a fantastic opportunity. I was lucky to be in the right place at the right time.

Having got official political blessing we started work later in 1976, first of all gathering information so that we had something to go on. The extent of the area was quite easy to agree, south of Clerkenwell Road in Islington, up to the Borough boundary with Camden, west of the Golden Lane Estate and the Barbican, and north of Holborn Viaduct and the St Paul's precinct in the City. It formed almost a square chunk of land with the enormous meat market running east-west right across the middle, from Farringdon Road virtually to Barbican Station on Aldersgate Street.

Both authorities had comprehensive land-use and employment records of every building in their patch for 1971/72. The immediate task was to compare this with 1976. The number crunching produced some startling results, which confirmed our worries. While employment within the market itself appeared fairly stable, at about 2,700, there had been a dramatic decline of 17 per cent in industrial jobs elsewhere in the area, and 35 per cent of all industrial and commercial floor space was now empty, up from 8 per cent in 1972. The survey showed that 28 per cent of those working in the market and industrial firms lived within inner London, compared to only 8 per cent of office-based workers. The number of people living within the area had also shrunk, from 1,300 in 1961 to 1,000 in 1971 and to only 800 in 1976. Most of these too were nurses in St Bartholomew's Hospital, and on the Islington side the community of gentlemen pensioners in the Charterhouse.

My assistant and colleague at Islington was Len Harris, an excellent and enthusiastic companion when we visited the meat market at night to see first-hand how it operated. We met at 10 p.m. on a cold, late autumn evening, by which time scores of big lorries were being skilfully manoeuvred into place around the edge of the market on Charterhouse Street,

Lindsey Street, Poultry Avenue and West Smithfield. Most of the heavy juggernauts had come from far afield, Ireland, Scotland and Wales, but also plenty were from Europe. During the day many of these forty-ton trucks had been lying up in St John Street or other side streets further north in Islington, where their rumbling refrigeration motors greatly annoyed the neighbours.

After a warming drink we went to the Market Office, where the genial Superintendent Douglas Noakes was to be our guide. He explained that before the war 80 per cent of the meat sold at Smithfield had come through the London or Liverpool docks, as much as 330,000 tons in 1938. By 1975 this had dwindled to only 50,000 tons, less than a quarter of the meat sold at Smithfield. The 1967 foot and mouth scare had virtually put paid to imports from Argentina, while Britain's membership in the European Economic Community since 1973 was squeezing out traditional Commonwealth produce.

Unloading started at midnight, enacted by gangs of men whose jobs were clearly demarcated, first the 'pullers-back', who dragged the meat to the tailboard, from where the 'pitchers' carried the carcasses into the market and onto the allotted rows of hooks hanging in the stalls. The pitchers often worked in pairs, synchronised like clockwork, to shoulder the long sides of beef, each weighing up to 180kg. Some pitchers half-ran with their cargo to minimise the strain. This, we were told, was the 'Smithfield shuffle'; eyes fixed, one arm swinging free, and blasphemy to anyone in the way.

Everything was carried by hand, exactly as it had been done for 100 years. Only in the Poultry Market were the pre-packed chickens carried on forklift trucks or rollers. Mr Noakes invited us to come again nearer to Christmas to see the festoons of turkeys, together with rabbit, hare and pheasant for the festive season.

By 4.00 a.m. the heavy lorries had been driven away and there was a temporary lull, time for another mug of steaming black tea laced with a generous slosh of whisky (known as 'wazzer' and highly recommended). The market was now full, a most splendid sight with row upon row of pigs, lambs, ewes, bullocks and calves hanging from their hooks. The 'shopmen' were now at work, weighing and checking the meat and improving the displays, while expert cutters were dismembering carcasses into more manageable joints for retail butchers. Severed heads were piled up for sale as brawn, and huge bins brimmed with livers, hearts or carefully folded strips of suet, all ready for the offal merchant. As he took us round, Mr Noakes proudly told us how every part of the animal would be sold to someone; nothing would go to waste. He introduced us to some of the seventy tenants, who between them rented the 230 stalls (still then on an insecure weekly basis). The biggest were Weddel's, Vestey's, Dewhurst and Thomas Borthwick, who owned Matthews, the high street butcher. Most outspoken was Peter Martinelli, who rented the coveted spot beside the central Grand Avenue, known as 'Peter's under the clock'. His business had expanded rapidly and he was keen on reform, modernisation, secure tenure and guaranteed rent levels, inducing a wry smile from the Superintendent.

Trading on the floor of the market started promptly at 5.00 a.m., wholesale only, a mysterious process where few prices were displayed and most of the haggling and bargaining among the assorted throng of agents and buyers was done by a nod and a wink. Outside, the lorries had been replaced by fleets of vans and smaller trucks.

The rules of the market allowed each buyer to take out only as much meat as he himself could carry in one journey. Official porters took the rest, piled high on wooden barrows to the awaiting vans, either working directly for the firms or carriers, or as self-employed 'bummarees', all licensed by the Market Superintendent. This was the most profitable work, piece-rate and cash on the nail. We were advised not to take photographs. Some of the bummarees were rough diamonds and any stranger with a camera might be suspected of being an undercover tax official or plain-clothed policeman.

Cowcross Street, 1976. (English Heritage)

Lots of the pubs were open by 6.00 a.m., such as the Cock Tavern in the market itself, but also many in the surrounding streets, ready to slake dry throats and take away the smell of blood and guts. We adjourned with Mr Noakes to the Fox and Anchor for a Smithfield breakfast. When we emerged blinking into the daylight at 8.00 a.m., most of the business was done, the market was almost empty and the vans had dispersed. Refuse vehicles were collecting the rubbish while men in waders hosed down the pavements and washed away the stench and sawdust.

Most of Smithfield's pubs were down-to-earth places, such as the Smithfield Tavern and the White Bear on the Islington side, and the Castle in Cowcross Street, still with its pawnbrokers' licence. On the City side, the Hand and Shears and the Old Red Cow were basic boozers. Sadly, the Rising Sun in Cloth Fair and White Horse in Little Britain had both closed, and the Globe at the bottom end of Hosier Lane was as derelict as its neighbours. The Barley Mow on Long Lane had reputedly been one of raffish Lord Lucan's haunts before his disappearance in 1974, perhaps because they did business lunches in a smart room upstairs.

Outside the market within our study area, there were 120 firms associated with the meat market, sausage-skin makers, ham and bacon curers, butchers' equipment shops and cold stores, employing over 3,000 people. There were even a handful of dealers in buttons, leather and tennis-racket gut, who once would have obtained their raw materials directly from the Smithfield slaughterhouses when, pre-1855, it was still a livestock market.

During our visits and meetings with a sample of these firms, Len and I found out that most were in serious decline. Hensons offal merchants had decided to move to Holloway because so much was being pilfered off the streets. Mr Church at Dumenil's in Cowcross Street explained how they could no longer compete with supermarkets for bacon and why they had stopped using the ancient smokeries tucked away behind White Horse Alley. Instead, they were now making hamburgers and chicken portions for restaurants and airlines, but thinking of moving closer to Heathrow. We learnt that Legrands and the game dealer Donald Sproat, both family firms handed down from father to son for generations, were on the verge of closure.

Mitchell & Inman, Cloth Fair. (Theo Bergström)

The reduction in imported meat from the docks had proved a death knell for the big cold stores, and most traders in the market now had their own smaller refrigerators. A trip round the recently closed Hedley Vicars' cold store revealed a catacomb of cork and melting ice. Most of the meat processing was contracting into the market itself, leaving mainly administrative functions in firms like Dewhurst, who retained offices in St John's Lane as much for the prestige and tradition of a Smithfield address as anything else.

Other local industries such as textiles, engineering and printing had employed over 4,500 people in 1972 but were declining even faster. Unsuitable premises, delivery problems for large vehicles in narrow streets and difficulties of recruiting local labour were all cited as reasons to move out. Once again we found some amazingly Dickensian survivors, Mitchell, Inman & Co. in Cloth Fair among them, huge rolls of cloth and felt stacked up on mahogany shelves, unchanged since 1800. Only the jewellery and craft trades seemed to be doing well.

The future of the meat market was of great concern to many. Some said that relocation on the lines of Covent Garden or what had happened in Paris when Les Halles Meat Market moved to La Villette in 1971 was unlikely, not only due to the cost but also because of vested interests. If Smithfield ceased functioning as a market it was rumoured that ownership of the land might revert from the Corporation back to the Crown. Nevertheless the market and its methods were antiquated, and probably in breach of new EEC hygiene legislation which required covered docking bays, stainless-steel floors and air-conditioning. Would the City Corporation meet the bill for these improvements or would the market simply wither away?

An Issues Paper in March 1977 was followed by a series of well-attended lunchtime and evening public meetings. After the publication of a draft plan in January 1978 and further consultation, the Smithfield Area Plan was finally agreed in June 1978. It strongly recommended retention and modernisation of the meat market, subsequently implemented by the Corporation. Less successfully it tried to protect local industry and to resist offices, although as a fall-back the idea of encouraging small studio-type offices rather than big office blocks was a good move.

The plan also highlighted the townscape value of the many fine Victorian commercial buildings in the area; factories, warehouses and cold stores, recognised their limitations for modern heavy industry and recommended a more flexible approach for their use. The conservation areas on the Islington side were extended to cover the whole area, and dozens of buildings were recommended for statutory listing. New policies were introduced to protect the views of the dome of St Paul's Cathedral from St John Street and Farringdon Road, the latter still blocked at that time by post-war monsters in Paternoster Square. Strict height limits for new building were defined along the sight lines, a method that would later be fed into Tim Catchpole's paper, London Skylines and the Department of the Environment's Strategic Planning Guidance for London. Perhaps it helped that he and I had been fellow students at the South Bank Poly.

New residential development was encouraged and a new housing scheme designed by Renton Howard Wood Levin was agreed for the north side of Cloth Fair, together with new hostels for St Bartholomew's Hospital and the medical school in Charterhouse Square. Bart's was almost as important to the area as the meat market, employing over 2,000 people. The GLC's Greater London Development Plan had unfortunately questioned whether 'so many facilities for medical teaching need to be in London' and 'whether the pressure on land for hospitals can be reduced'; not exactly encouraging words. The Smithfield Plan sought to cement Bart's historic place in the area. Besides, the juxtaposition of hospital and market was one of the great attributes of the area, trainee doctors and bummarees jostling for bar space in the Sutton Arms or the Hope. Whose actually were the white coats stained with blood?

After 1978, Islington and the City went their separate ways, but it sowed the seed for much which followed on the Islington side, designating the Industrial Improvement Area, new conservation areas, policies on building heights, design and mixed use. It paved the way not only for the regeneration of Clerkenwell, but a new renaissance in the inner city. When Alan Baxter moved his design office into Cowcross Street in 1979, very much a pioneer, it was a sure sign of things to come.

Having had some insight into so many remarkable institutions and seen so many layers of history, it struck me that this tiny area was London's most special 'faubourg'. Here was a district where a century ago people had lived, worked, shopped, been to school and church, and had amused themselves. By the 1970s that mix and balance had suffered. If only the full mosaic of human activity could be restored and enlivened, then Smithfield could regain its vitality. It seemed a good subject for a book.

✂ THE CITY ✂

The Smithfield study had given me a glimpse into the fabric and inner workings of the City and Corporation. We had regular meetings with our counterparts in their spacious and rather grand offices in the Guildhall. They even had security guards to check your bags, unheard of then in lowly Islington.

We had reached consensus on most things in the Smithfield Plan, even persuading the City to extend their conservation area in Cloth Fair to include Middle and Newbury Streets, but not on everything. Some things, they made clear, were none of Islington's business. The Corporation were still hell-bent on road improvements, one consequence of which was the outrageous demolition of the east end of the bomb-damaged Christchurch Newgate Street. This Wren church, with its lovely spire, had been left as a ruined shell after the war, and was not

Little Britain, 1978.
(English Heritage)

proposed for rebuilding. Its truncation in 1974, merely to enable vehicles to speed around the corner, was an act of wanton vandalism.

Much of Little Britain and the network of tiny courts and alleys to the rear were also threatened by a new road, and therefore not recommended for conservation area protection. This was all part of the so-called Route XI, already manifest in the dual-carriageway stretch of London Wall between Aldersgate Street and Moorgate. Even the Museum of London, designed by Powell and Moya and proudly opened in 1976, had been built around and on top of a giant roundabout, so that Route XI could continue westwards. In the way stood the forlorn buildings of Cross Keys Square, Cox's Court and Albion Buildings. Postman's Park was to be spared, and a façade of buildings on Little Britain itself, but nothing would change the Corporation's mind.

Route XI had its supporters, not least Sir Nikolaus Pevsner, who had said of London Wall: 'It promises to be of high aesthetic value and London's most advanced concept of central area development.' (He also misguidedly praised the Knightsbridge Barracks on the edge of Hyde Park.) Of the road, he said: 'The only pity is that the whole of London Wall is so short. No sooner have you stepped on the gas than you have to brake because you have reached the Aldersgate end'.

Route XI was part of the post-war plan to build a ring road around the City, which also involved the construction of the semi-motorway of Upper and Lower Thames Street, linking the Victoria Embankment with Tower Bridge. Within this necklace of fast roads the idea was to segregate vehicles and pedestrians vertically, and to create a network throughout the Square Mile of elevated walkways above the traffic, called 'ped-ways'. The policy had been cemented in 1963 with a requirement for all future development to incorporate this feature, and meant that most buildings had to have two entrances, one to serve the new 'ped-way' and an interim one at ground level. The wise but insular City Fathers and their planning officers, no doubt envisaged that in time the whole of the City would be rebuilt, perhaps with the exception of St Paul's and the Guildhall. They weren't thinking much beyond the City boundaries.

By the mid-1970s opposition to this lunacy was mounting. In 1976, 'SAVE THE CITY' was published jointly by the Society for the Protection of Ancient Buildings, the Georgian Group, the

Victorian Society and the Civic Trust. Their report was presented both to the City Corporation and to a wider public as a basis for conserving the City's unique character without prejudicing its outstanding international role as a financial centre. The authors, mainly David Lloyd and Jennifer Freeman, but with contributions from many others, did much to change hearts and minds in some quarters. In any event, the wretched 'ped-way' system was abandoned in the late 1970s.

Coming from Islington, where apart from government-funded public housing it was proving difficult to attract any form of private property investment, things in the City were very different and pressure for development was intense. The husband of clarinettist Betty happened to be the site foreman and senior engineer for Mowlem's, who were building Richard Seifert's magnum opus, the new tower for the National Westminster Bank on Old Broad Street. At fifty-two storeys and almost exactly 600ft, it was set to be the highest building in Britain. On a rather alarmingly windy day in November 1977, Steve invited me to visit the site, to enjoy the thrill of climbing to the top in a precarious external wire cage. From the unprotected roof above the completed central core, the rest of the City and the whole of London lay below us. Steve told me how during a gale two weeks previously, an unsecured aluminium ladder had blown off in the middle of the night and landed several streets away, luckily harming no one.

There were plenty of cranes breaking the City skyline. To the east was Cutlers Gardens, while to the south there was a clutch of new developments near the river and Cannon Street Station. Of these Mondial House was attracting the most comment, a new state-of-the-art exchange for the International Telephone Service, right on the river between Fishmongers' Hall and the station. The architects, Hubbard Ford, had recently designed the relatively contextual brick-clad hotel at Queenhithe (although sadly knocking down some fine Victorian warehouses in the process). Mondial House was not only bombproof but almost shockingly non-contextual, its concrete clad in shiny glass-reinforced polyester. At best, from across the river it looked like a colossal computer keyboard, and the paddle-steamer *Princess Elizabeth* moored in front of it lent an incongruous

Mondial House from London Bridge, 1975. (Geoffrey Pearce)

The Mansion House site, Mappin & Webb, 1979. (English Heritage)

charm. This was part of the 1970s fad for converting nautical relics into floating bars or restaurants, started by the success of Tattershall Castle further along the Embankment in 1972.

The street frontage of Cannon Street Station itself was also being startlingly rebuilt by Arup Associates, with the stainless steel structure exposed externally as a giant lattice across fashionable dark glass. The busiest architects in the City, however, were Fitzroy Robinson & Partners. They were at the forefront of introducing the idea of deep-plan, big floor-plate, air-conditioned offices from America, notably at Aldgate House, completed in 1976. In Leadenhall Street, their new 1978 building for the Institute of London Underwriters included an atrium, another novel concept at the time, much copied.

The 1970s also witnessed a move away from the exposed concrete and external mosaic tiling clichés of the '60s, and introduced a new fashion for polished stone cladding, exotic marbles, granites and limestones. Sometimes this was excellent and appropriate, such as in the Banque National de Paris in King William Street, again by Fitzroy Robinson, but often it resulted in flat, bland and unrelieved elevations, as in Cutlers Gardens.

The greatest controversy in the City, which rumbled right through the entire decade, was Lord Palumbo's Mansion House proposal to redevelop a site at the junction of Poultry and Queen Victoria Street with an eighteen-storey tower designed by Mies van der Rohe. Problems of land acquisition and mounting objections eventually delayed and blocked that scheme, and instead it was the redevelopment of Lloyd's of London in Leadenhall Street which was to produce the City's most celebrated and innovative building. Although Richard Rogers' high-tech masterpiece wasn't finished until well into the 1980s, it was designed in the 1970s, borrowing much from his Pompidou Centre in Paris and in so doing put the City on the international architectural map.

The gigantic Barbican complex, begun in the 1950s, was still under construction, most notably the Arts Centre, scheduled to open in 1982. The new adjacent premises for the Guildhall School of Music and Drama (GSMD), also by Chamberlin, Powell & Bon, opened in 1977, thus vacating their beloved old building in John Carpenter Street.

I had fond memories of the old GSMD, having spent many an hour rehearsing in its resonant practice rooms. Now its echoing corridors were silent. The neighbourhood, however, was still dominated by the printers and offices of the newspaper industry, and their watering holes. Although the disastrous bombing of the war had resulted in most of the publishing houses which had clustered in the EC4 postal district, relocating to Mayfair and Bloomsbury, where 'temporary' office permissions had been given in Georgian houses, the newspapers and journals remained firmly concentrated in Fleet Street. In the 1970s only a few moved out, *The Times* (owned then by Lord Northcliffe) to Gray's Inn Road and the *Guardian* to Farringdon Road. The *Observer*, still independent, remained in Tudor Street. Rupert Murdoch owned only the *Sun*, and hadn't yet embarked on his crusade to smash the unions and move his operations to 'fortress Wapping'. Nor was Robert Maxwell, owner of Pergamon Press, much involved with newspapers then; the *Mirror* was still owned by Reed International.

From midday onwards and late into the night, the network of tiny streets south of Fleet Street buzzed with activity. Lorries delivered huge rolls of paper onto loading bays, the clatter and fumes of hot metal filled the air, and the pubs roared with argument and laughter. This was the age when people became legends in their own lunchtimes.

By 1976, my school friend Jonny was working for Post Office Telecommunications (the precursor of British Telecom) in their premises near Smithfield. Between us we hatched the excellent plan of visiting, each time we met for a lunchtime pint, one of the fifty-plus City of London churches. One-hour lunches on Fridays became somewhat stretched, but my bike made it possible, and Jonny's offices at Nos 2-12 Gresham Street were also known as 12-2.

The task was clearly not going to be completed quickly, but armed with John Betjeman's wonderful eponymous guide, published in 1974 under Pitkin's *Pride of Britain* series, we set to work. With respectful diligence, we always did the church first.

Smithfield was a good place to start, at St Bartholomew-the-Great and the Bishop's Finger, and then St Sepulchre's and the White Hart in Giltspur Street. From St Ethelburga's in Ely Place we found Ye Olde Mitre even more hidden away in Ely Court. And so we progressed around the City, meeting about once a month. It was a good way to get to know the back alleys, savouring the delights of the Black Friar, Ye Olde Cheshire Cheese off Fleet Street and Ye Olde Watling near the Mansion House, the Britannia in Fish Street Hill, the Cockpit in St Andrew's Hill, the Golden Fleece in Queen Street and the East India Arms in Fenchurch Street. Among our architectural favourites were the Lord Aberconway at the north end of Old Broad Street and the Lamb in Leadenhall Market, both of which had mezzanine seating galleries above the bar. The City certainly retained some remarkably historic pub interiors, as Roderick Gradidge so passionately expounded in SAVE THE CITY, and some of them were under threat. The venerable black timber panelling of Old Wine Shades in Martin Lane was only preserved after a bitter planning battle in 1972. Everywhere there was pressure for change, fruit machines and cigarette dispensers, open-plan bars, flashing lights and plush banquettes to replace settles and benches.

As well as enjoying the Bank of England's superb sports' facilities at Roehampton, I also regularly met Gordon for lunch in the City. He had started working for the bank in 1973, with Gordon Richardson as Governor, and although it had a luxurious staff canteen to deter its workforce from leaving the building, it too seemed to tolerate a relaxed regime on timekeeping. We invariably went to Simpson's in Castle Court off Cornhill, a traditional chop house where we bought our beer at the tiny ground-floor bar and then went up the narrow stairs to eat in the steamy dining room. We sat on high-backed oak pews, all with polished brass coat hooks, and ate stewed cheese, braised hearts, jam roly-poly or spotted dick and custard, all washed down with copious glass tankards of the best draught Bass in London. The mature uniformed waitresses were from the molly-coddling school of matrons, but quick and efficient when necessary, chatty and flirty when not. The whole place was a Dickensian delight before it was renovated in 1980.

While bowler hats, brollies and briefcases might have been disappearing fast from City streets, the pin-stripe suit, college tie and the old-boy network was as strong as ever, in which the long liquid lunch played an important part. In the 1970s the yuppie hadn't been invented. A few posers sported the latest Filo-Fax or Pulsar wristwatch, but no one yet had a mobile phone, not even the proto-type 'bricks' which arrived in the 1980s. The City was old-fashioned, closely regulated, and the unchallenged master of its own world. Nothing, it seemed, could change that.

∾ THE REGENT'S CANAL ∾

I had first seen the Regent's Canal as a child on a visit to the zoo. Snuggled in its gentle cutting between the green spaces of Primrose Hill and Regent's Park, it seemed to be a pleasant piece of waterway, with a well-maintained pathway, protected by railings from the water's edge. There were ducks and moorhens to be fed, and I thought no more about it than I did the lakes in Regent's Park itself. Only when I came to live in London did I find more pieces of this same canal and wonder where it went.

Unlike the River Thames, which was an unmissable feature, the canal was quite the opposite, remarkably hidden away from public gaze for much of its tortuous path through North London. In the winter of 1973, I began to explore with my brother the section either side from Camden Lock, more properly known then as the Hampstead Road Locks. Westwards, we marvelled at the way the canal threaded a passage under the Euston railway lines, past the huge dilapidated remains of the Camden Goods Station and coal store, all connected to the canal by docks and inlets. We admired the bulk of the Gilbey's gin-bottling works and the old ice house at Jamieson Road, and how, beyond the Oval Road, it suddenly transformed into the familiar

Above left: City Road Basin, looking north from City Road bridge, 1975. (Geoffrey Pearce)

Above right: East of Mare Street bridge, Hackney, looking back to the gasworks, 1975. (Geoffrey Pearce)

Regent's Canal lock, Limehouse Basin, London & Blackwall railway viaduct, 1979. (English Heritage)

Primrose Hill section, where weeping willows and verdant gardens of handsome villas sprawled down to the canal's edge.

While the canal itself had seemingly lost its commercial lifeblood and raison d'être, the potential attraction of a canal-side setting was clearly apparent to the colonisers of Dingwalls and Camden Lock. In 1977, near the Oval Road bridge overlooking the canal, Richard Seifert designed what was probably his most playful structure, the Pirate Castle children's centre.

Eastwards we pondered the fate of the derelict Henly's garage (demolished in 1980 for the TV-am studios and Terry Farrell's famous egg cups) and the Art Deco Aerated Bread Co. factory. As the canal snaked its way beneath five road bridges, the tow path and its retaining walls were choked with buddleia, and the run-down sheds, yards and warehouses alongside St Pancras Way were protected with festoons of brambles and barbed-wire.

Our destination was the spectacular landscape of King's Cross, the cluster of gas holders and the backdrop of the spires of St Pancras Station. Here there were dozens of abandoned buildings, including the Great Northern Railway coal drops, which were soon to be demolished and provide the site for the Camley Street nature reserve. No one yet had put up any information signs to explain the rope-worn grooves cut into the stone bridge abutments or the ramp descending into the water near the St Pancras railway bridge, put there so that terrified horses who had been frightened into the water by passing steam trains could get out again. All the road bridges over the canal, including the Maiden Lane bridge on York Way, had high brick walls which prevented pedestrians seeing over, and there were very few access points down to the towpath at King's Cross. Any progress by foot further east was thwarted by the stately western portal of the long Islington tunnel.

Arriving to work in Islington, I began to learn much more about the canal, greatly assisted by the deep knowledge and fascination for its history and preservation by my Planning Department colleague Geoff Gribble. Horn-playing Howard, with whom I'd travelled to Austria and who worked for YRM Architects in Clerkenwell, rented a top-floor flat on Noel Road, overlooking the canal, the so-called 'hanging gardens' of Islington.

During most of the 1970s the British Waterways Board (BWB), who owned the canal and its towpath, seemed intent on running it down, rather like British Rail with the railways. In 1975 all the second chambers of the double locks downstream from Camden Town were converted to weirs, as much to save water as a reflection of the almost complete absence of barge traffic. Even public access to the towpath was a debatable issue, particularly when a deal was done with the Central Electricity Generating Board (CEGB) to run high-voltage cables under the towpath. For a time in 1976 it seemed possible that the towpath might disappear altogether.

Luckily there were some stout campaigners and visionaries. At King's Cross, many of the fine brick-built warehouses around Battlebridge Basin were under threat. In 1973 the Victorian Westinghouse on the north-west corner had been demolished and replaced by an ugly red-brick shed. It seemed that the vacant Porter's bottling works might suffer the same fate, together with Gatti's Wharf, Albert Wharf and Pembroke Wharf. No enlightened developers were on hand in the 1970s to invest in refurbishment and alternative uses for these buildings. There was even talk of filling in the basin altogether. Fortunately a group of enthusiasts, including John Yates, had started living there on a collection of narrow boats and formed a permanent mooring. The rent they paid and the fuss they created perhaps helped to steer BWB on a different course.

East of the Islington tunnel, City Road Basin was also threatened. Here a local resident, Crystal Hale, daughter of Sir Alan (A.P.) Herbert, took up the cudgels. Having moved in 1968 into her house on Noel Road, backing onto the canal near the delightful Hanover School, she founded the Islington Boat Club in 1970 and began using the disused City Road Basin, mainly for canoes. Despite the decrepit nature of the commercial surroundings, it soon became a magnet for local children, and an inspiration to youth workers. Jim Armstrong, who worked there in the summer of 1975, said that it changed his life, and he went on to start the Laburnum Boat Club at Haggerston.

The London Canals Committee was set up to protect the canal and its basins, and to try to encourage sympathetic development along its banks. Newly formed local groups such as the Islington Narrow Boat Association helped the cause. It was even suggested that the Planning Department should produce a development brief to guide future building around City Road basin. How about a footbridge across the locks and a new towpath around the basin itself? With the Diespeker terrazzo factory and its elegant chimney lying empty, and the CEGB owning much of the land around the basin, the immediate prospects seemed bleak. The Angel Canal Festival was still a few years off.

Further east into Hackney, beyond the Narrow Boat pub at the Wharf Road bridge, the canal was even bleaker. This was a sliver of London which not many people sought to discover. It had its own peculiar beauty; reflections in the ripples, water gushing through leaking lock gates, the long views punctuated by gas works and chimneys such as the Regent's Canal Ironworks at Eagle Wharf Road. But exploration was also tinged with a sense of unease. Walking the towpath here was not for the faint-hearted, even in broad daylight; the canal was full of unsavoury rubbish, possibly the odd corpse, not a soul to be seen except the occasional guard dog, barking madly behind a wire fence, itching to sink its fangs into the nearest available flesh. And everywhere there was dereliction, broken glass and graffiti.

Victoria Park provided some respite, the comfort of being overlooked by houses and gardens, and then came the choice to turn north-east up the Hertfordshire Union Canal towards the Lea Valley or south-west towards Limehouse. Here, vast areas which hadn't been bombed in the Blitz were being cleared for the new Mile End Park, but the job was as yet far from complete. It was a desolate and fractured landscape.

Spookiest of all was the Limehouse Cut, running from Limehouse Basin to the River Lea at Bromley-by-Bow. Here, every factory and warehouse seemed to turn its back on the canal. Although the canal ran straight and you could see any trouble ahead on the towpath, you were trapped and there was no escape other than to turn around. A bicycle always seemed the safest bet to make a quick retreat.

✎ DOCKLANDS ✎

Following the canal was as good a way as any to find London's docklands, emerging from under the magnificent bridge of George and Robert Stephenson into the huge expanse of Limehouse Basin. The claustrophobia of the canal was now replaced by vast open spaces. The decline of London's docklands was no surprise, but the sheer extent of the area involved certainly was.

Gun Wharves, Wapping High Street, 1973. (English Heritage)

The growth of containerisation and bigger ships which needed deep-water ports had sounded the death knell for London docks. The opening of the new container port at Tilbury in 1968, together with the expanding facilities at Felixstowe, brought a dramatic reduction in cargo to London. The 1970 and 1972 National Dock strikes turned out to be futile gestures which only made things worse. During the 1970s the number of jobs directly employed in the docks shrank from 29,000 to just over 2,000. Associated industries and businesses were equally hard hit. Between 1966 and 1976, over 100,000 jobs were lost in the five dockland Boroughs, over one-fifth of the work force.

After passing a pretty group of old houses beside the river on Narrow Street, we entered the Isle of Dogs and cycled the circuit round West Ferry Road, Manchester Road and Preston Road, stopping to admire the view across to Greenwich at the southern tip. Everywhere was virtually deserted. Through gaps and open gates in the periphery walls we could see the idle cranes and gantries of the West India and Millwall Docks. Nor was there much apparent security and it looked as though you could wander around much as you pleased.

Along the way there were a few pockets of bleak inter-war housing, not a tree in sight, and a few unlikely looking pubs, such as the Pier Tavern and Cubitt Arms, for all the world like lessons in temperance. At Blackwall we came to the East India Dock and the grim wastelands of Leamouth Road. Further east beyond Bow Creek and the muddy waters of the River Lea lay the even bigger Royal Docks, stretching as far as the eye could see.

The terrible plight of the area had provoked the neglected residents of the Isle of Dogs to proclaim independence in 1970, inspired by the Ealing comedy *Passport to Pimlico*. Whether serious or comic, it did draw attention to the vacuum in both economic activity and any proper planning for the future. David Eversley, chief strategic planner in the GLC, commissioned Travers Morgan to prepare proposals for the eight sq. miles of docklands, mainly based on provision of public housing rather than new employment.

The host of different landowners – the Port of London Authority (PLA), British Rail, the British Gas Corporation, the CEGB, the GLC and the different London Boroughs – all

St Katharine Dock, 1972. (Theo Bergström)

with their own agendas, meant that a coordinated plan never made it off the drawing board. In 1974 the Docklands Joint Committee was set up, to include the GLC and the Boroughs, but little progress was made apart from piecemeal developments. The City Corporation eyed up a site beside West India Dock as a potential place to relocate Billingsgate Fish Market.

Meanwhile some of the docks struggled on. By 1978 the financial losses had brought the PLA to the brink of insolvency. The Labour government, in desperation, pumped in £35 million in return for promises of manpower reduction and changes in working practices. There were further local strikes, urged on by the militant communist trade union leader Jack Dash. The money almost literally drained away. In 1980 the West India and Millwall Docks finally closed, although they'd been effectively dead for years. The Royal Docks closed a year later, leaving 6,000 acres in need of regeneration. 'Docklands in the Doldrums' was how *The Times* put it.

Some believed that St Katharine Dock, close to the Tower of London, provided the answer. This had closed in 1968 and been developed by Taylor Woodrow, advertised as a 'new Venice', more mundanely a marina and potential tourist magnet. Unfortunately the ugly new Thistle Hotel and World Trade Centre buildings designed by Renton Howard Wood in 1973 and 1976 didn't improve the setting of the docks or the Tower of London, but several of the old warehouses were restored and the locks and quays repaired. The Dickens Inn was concocted out of recycled timbers, a fake fantasy which added to the folksy image. St Katharine Dock, in any event, was just 200 acres, tiny compared to the greater problem at large.

Immediately to the east, Wapping had its attractions, the cobbled carriageways which turned bikes into bone-shakers and the vertiginous empty warehouses which made canyons of the High Street and Wapping Wall. The Town of Ramsgate and the Prospect of Whitby pubs were close enough to the City to lure Gordon and I on the occasional sunny summer lunchtime, and were as yet unknown to tourists. To the north lay the abandoned Shadwell Basin and Tobacco Dock. The absence of any plans or ideas for their re-use led to the tragic demolition in 1979 of the mighty North Stack warehouse (dating from 1805), which would later provide the site for Murdoch's News International, and bring Wapping very forcibly into the headlines.

Having reached Limehouse Basin by canal, there was as yet no possibility of a circular return trip by a riverside path, although no doubt the planners were working on it. Instead, after a pint in the Grapes in Narrow Street, we cut up to the Commercial Road and diverted briefly into York Square, a delightful enclave of early Victorian two-storey terraces which had miraculously escaped bombs and bulldozers. We'd been tipped off by the 1976 *Good Beer Guide's* entry for the Queen's Head on the junction of Flamborough and Chaseley Streets, 'a comfortable pub in a redevelopment area'. The GLC had indeed been buying up property and land from the Mercers' Co.; the new Watney Market Estate, finished in 1975 just down the road, was one result. York Square had been acquired in 1973 but happily the GLC chose to refurbish. The Queen's Head and the Ship in the opposite corner of the square merited return visits. On Sunday lunchtimes there was free seafood at the bar and the place was packed with East End stereotypes. Half-jokingly we thought it would be good material for a soap opera. At least the GLC were doing their bit to sustain Wilmott and Young's *Family and Kinship in the East End*, even if the regeneration of the docks, the spirit of free enterprise and the cult of *EastEnders* would have to wait for the next decade.

Soon after it was published in 1977 I was given a copy of Gillian Tyndall's *The Fields Beneath: The History of One London Village*. Her scholarship, coupled with a very readable style, gave me a fresh insight into a part of North London which I thought I'd got to know and showed me that local history, if well written, could be gripping stuff.

Kentish Town had seemed to me to be one of those 'in between' areas beyond Camden, rather like Holloway is to Islington. Parts of it were semi-industrial and rough, although the sign for the scrap metal dealers McWeeney & Smallman, next to the Gospel Oak railway, always raised a smile. The Kentish Town City Farm, started in 1972 on railway land near Grafton Road, was an endearing addition, the first of its type in London, and a welcome relief to the unrelenting blocks of Council flats being built on Mansfield Road, designed by Frederick McManus.

Estate agents tried their best to call parts of the area Tufnell Park or Dartmouth Park, and some people living in The Grove or Little Green Street reckoned they were 'Highgate borders', but the streets either side of the High Street were inescapably Kentish Town. Being closer to the Heath and the trendiness of Camden Town it was more appealing than Holloway, and because Camden Council had been less active than Islington in buying up ordinary terraced housing, there was more private property on the market.

I had first been there as a teenager to Jim and Paul Howarth's house in Montpelier Grove, accompanied by my father and uncle, to buy a clarinet. Even though the Howarths had retail premises in the West End in Blandford Street, for some reason we went to their house, perhaps because it was closer to my uncle's flat in Chalk Farm. Montpelier Grove was a typically grimy street, windows draped with torn net curtains, dustbins on the pavement and not a tree to be seen.

Woolworth's, Kentish Town Road, 1978. (English Heritage)

When two friends, Roger and Shantee, moved into a rented flat in Falkland Road in 1975, some of the streets were showing signs of gentrification, particularly the pretty southern end of Leverton Street and the cottages in Fortess Grove. While most of the main-road pubs were unappealing and sold an unattractive range of keg beers, the Pineapple in Leverton Street was a delightfully unspoilt backstreet local, full of good-humoured regulars drinking light and bitter and newcomers like us quaffing the Taylor-Walker and Burton ales.

Kentish Town Road had some eye-catching shops; Buston's Coats and Gowns and Dawson & Briant's jewellers, a relic from another age. Best of all was the thriving Owl Bookshop, which was loyally supported by the local community. Chamberlain's was also one of the largest bicycle retailers in North London, but not so good for repairs. In Fortess Road was Phelps' Pianos, a survivor from the once-enormous North London piano industry.

The proximity of all the Greek tavernas in Camden Town was stiff competition for anyone setting up a restaurant, but the Bengal Lancer was a good bet for a reliable, if unspectacular, curry. The hidden gem was Le Petit Prince which opened in 1979 in Holmes Road, replacing the dingy Zenith restaurant, which had reached its nadir. The space inside was tiny, with room for just half-a-dozen tables, but they served the best merguez and couscous in town. The Spaghetti House Café, near the corner of Dartmouth Park Hill and Fortess Road, was also wonderfully cheap and let you take in your own booze.

One odd story about the shops concerned the retrieval of a stolen bassoon from a colleague in the Forest Philharmonic. In desperation, Glyn had gone to a clairvoyant who reckoned she could 'see it' somewhere for sale in Kentish Town, and there in a junk shop in Fortess Road he found it.

When I started to look for somewhere to buy, Kentish Town seemed a good bet, cheaper than the Georgian terraces of Islington. Stickley & Kent sent me details of several houses, in Patshull Road, Lawford Road and Leighton Road, but I'd missed the boat. The thirty-something barristers and solicitors who'd been buying up run-down properties since the early 1970s in Camden Square or Lady Somerset Road had forced up the prices to beyond what I could afford. These were the people who referred to Kentish Town Road as 'the village' and probably, most laudably, patronised the Owl Bookshop. My long-standing dream of buying and living somewhere within walking distance of Hampstead Heath was not going to be realised and I had to get used to that fast.

ꙮ HOLLOWAY ꙮ

In 1975 my brother had moved to Bath and, after renting a lovely second-floor flat in The Circus, he bought a three-storey Victorian terraced house in 1976 for about £10,000. This went down well with my parents, who always regarded rent as 'money down the drain'. I started to think about getting a foot on a rung of the property ladder. Apart from the fantasy of Vanbrugh Castle, I hadn't done much about it, but now I realised that there was a danger of missing out.

I had heard tales of people buying run-down houses in Barnsbury in the late '60s and early '70s for just a few thousand pounds, but I was too late for that. Inflation had taken such properties way beyond my reach, with house prices going up by 36 per cent nationally in 1973 alone, probably more in central London.

I let one golden opportunity slip through my fingers when I was told that the Church Cottage beside St Mary's churchyard off Upper Street might be for sale. On the planning file I found the beautiful coloured-linen drawings of Seeley and Paget, who had restored both the

Windsor Road, 1979. No. 70 far left with cornice, No. 73 stone-clad. (Author's Collection)

cottage and the parish church after war damage. Now the diocese was selling it off, apparently for offers over £4,000. I dithered and the chance was gone. In November 1976 I went to see a shabby four-storey house in Gerrard Road, near the Angel and the canal, with butler sinks on the landings, smelly carpets and an outside toilet. It was on the market for £21,000 and needed renovation. With an annual salary of £3,500 and the normal maximum mortgage offer only three times that, South Islington was out of my league.

I turned towards North Islington, an area I knew only patchily. As a teenager and student I had taken lessons with William Waterhouse, co-principal bassoonist with Geoffrey Gambold in the BBC Symphony Orchestra and member of the Melos Ensemble. I was familiar with the trudge up Highgate Hill from Archway tube station to his house in Cromwell Avenue, just over the Borough boundary in Haringey. After at least two hours of listening to Bill's reminiscences, both musical and archaeological, and a bit of bassoon playing, I would canter back down the hill towards the grey Archway towers and the belching fumes of the traffic maelstrom at the roundabout.

In the summer of 1976 I'd worked on proposals to create a new park by demolishing houses in Alexander and Landseer Roads, north of Seven Sisters Road, a part of the Borough with the least amount of public open space. My friends Paddy and Di lived on the smarter west side of Holloway Road in one of the pretty Tavistock Terrace cottages with funny moulded heads over the front doors, and they enthused about Holloway.

Armed with the particulars from Stickley & Kent I went to see No. 70 Windsor Road on 30 May 1977, a surprisingly pleasant side street north of the Nag's Head Shopping Centre, and sufficiently far from the junction with Holloway Road to escape the worst of its roar. The long three-storey terrace on the north side of the street also had the merit of being flat-fronted, without projecting ground-floor bays. To my eyes, although the street was Victorian it more closely resembled my Georgian ideal. Bays looked fussy and besides, they had a nasty habit of falling away from the rest of the house.

The man in the Leeds Permanent Building Society office round the corner offered a mortgage of £10,500, but also an additional £2,500 advance which was secured by a guarantee from the father of my Kensington flatmate Robin, who was keen to move too as a lodger.

His generous father also paid two years' rent up front. That, coupled with my own savings from three cheap years in Queen's Gate Terrace, did the trick.

One lodger was not enough to pay the cripplingly high interest rates (even with the tax relief on mortgage interest repayments introduced by Roy Jenkins). Neil and Elspeth, house-sitting in Abbey Gardens, St John's Wood, for the Cruft family, were on the lookout and decided that Holloway was a good option. By the time I picked up the keys on 7 October, Neil had shacked up with his girlfriend Hannah, while sister Elspeth went elsewhere. Neil, Hannah, Robin and I moved in the next day.

The vendors were a young couple going their separate ways. In the confusion of their departure, piles of their stuff were left behind, mainly junk and soiled clothes, but also a life-size and strikingly lifelike toy chimp. We found him sitting forlornly on the steep narrow stairs to the maid's closet above the top floor landing. Although he wasn't actually a piece of taxidermy, and had artificial hair, he was convincing enough to have come from Get Stuffed on Essex Road. Monkey became part of the family.

With Neil and Robin as drinking companions we explored the local pubs, which were high in number but disappointingly low in the provision of good real ale. Many were old-fashioned Irish fighting pubs run by surly or red-faced landlords, ready to quell any Friday-night nonsense with knuckledusters hanging on the back bar next to the optics. We soon found the Admiral Mann, tucked away in Hargrave Place off Brecknock Road, a delightful gem with two tiny rooms and a jug-and-bottle off-sales counter, serving McMullen's Country bitter and AK mild, well worth the fifteen-minute walk. They provided the firkin for our housewarming party, seventy-two pints for £21.

Hannah was a more unusual and serious-minded housemate, having worked as an expert chef running the kitchen of the successful Spread Eagle in Greenwich, but now afflicted by blistered corneas in her eyes and facing potential blindness. Unable to continue as a professional cook she took to writing about food for the *New Statesman* and started working as a volunteer in the St John's Way Day Centre near Archway. Neil was also a good cook, so we ate well. Hannah continued to mastermind the occasional institutional banquet, at Westminster Medical School for example, when it was all hands to the pump.

The house itself was nothing special, but in tolerable condition. The bathroom was antiquated, but at least had a bath with hot and cold running water, and the night-storage heaters were better than nothing. We occasionally flouted the 1968 Clean Air Act by enjoying an open fire and lighting a bonfire. The tiny front garden housed the bins behind a privet hedge and the modest back yard was overshadowed by the looming bulk of the National Savings Bank offices on Manor Gardens. No. 70 was the last house going east to retain its cornice, the others having been blown off when a German V1 rocket fell in 1944, creating the space where Bennett Court was subsequently built. Our neighbours next door at No. 69 remembered it well. Les and Flo Soley had lived there since 1936, he having been a policeman on duty when the bomb landed. Now hard of hearing, they lived in quiet retirement with their overweight dog, Mac, spending most of their time in the back scullery, which still had an earth floor. Flo made Les smoke his pipe outside, and on Saturdays he sloped off to watch Tottenham Hotspur.

Having rejected my uncle's piano when he'd left Chalk Farm, I now had the space to house more than an upright. Thanks to a small ad in the *Cambridge Evening News*, I bought an Ibach grand for £300 from some honeymooners who had inherited it and wanted to be shot of it. Somehow the removers got it up the stairs to the first-floor front room. Elspeth came to tune and regulate it; homespun chamber music and homemade beer-making flourished.

In search of a refrigerator, an *Evening Standard* ad led us in our hired Telson's van to a very grand mansion in Maida Vale and the residence of Francis Hovell-Thurlow-Cumming-Bruce,

8th Baron Thurlow, one-time Governor of the Bahamas and High Commissioner to New Zealand. His jolly wife flogged us the fridge for £10 and then offered us two wonderfully large and comfortable armchairs and a standard lamp, thrown in for free. They were, she explained while her husband demurely poured the drinks, 'having a clear out'.

We quickly grew to like the good things about living in Holloway. There genuinely did seem to be more of an established community than in Kensington, not only because of the Soleys, but in the friendliness of many of the local shopkeepers, whether Irish, Cypriot, Italian or cockney. Gibber's greengrocers on Seven Sisters Road had an excellent selection of fruit and vegetables, not quite the rival of Brixton but it had rock-bottom prices. Matthews & Dewhurst butchers on Holloway (not yet taken over by Corrigan's) bought their meat every morning from Smithfield Market. Hannah even tried to persuade Scott's Electric Bakery to sell more wholemeal bread, part of her campaign against the poor quality white-sliced pulp produced by the corporate giants. Richards was a good fishmonger on Seven Sisters Road, with Caribbean red snapper, flying fish and shark alongside the normal. Best of all was Gerra & Sons at No. 85 Parkhurst Road for everything Italian – cheese, salami and olives – and always a cheery 'Hello, Meesta'. Even the cashiers in the Midland Bank on the corner with Hercules Street were good-natured.

Holloway's flagship store was Jones Bros, part of the John Lewis partnership. It was the perfect place to buy curtains and cup hooks for the house, and had a touch of class which James Selby's shop lacked. It seemed unthinkable in 1977 that John Lewis would eventually cull all its suburban department stores and that Jones Bros would suffer the same fate as John Barnes in Finchley Road and Pratts in Streatham.

The supermarkets weren't so hot. On the other corner with Tollington Road and on the site of the magnificent Beale's restaurant and bakery, demolished in 1970, was a downmarket Sainsbury's in a horrible dark brick shed. No better was the Safeway's in Seven Sisters

Holloway Thanksgiving supper, 24 November 1977. (Author's Collection)

Road, opposite Gibber's, which seemed to stock more dog food than anything else. Next door, Argos had opened in 1974, one of the first of Richard Tomkins' new chain. Tomkins had already established Green Shield Stamp shops, where people traded in their stamps for goods. Apparently while on holiday in the Greek town of Argos, he had the bright idea of not bothering any more with stamps and using cash instead. 'Buy it at Argos and pocket the difference' was the slogan, later changed to 'Famous names at unheard of prices'.

In 1976, McDonald's opened in Seven Sisters Road (only their second outlet in London after the first in Woolwich), and offered a burger, fries and Coke for 49p. The previous year an open-air market had started on a vacant site near the Nag's Head pub on Seven Sisters Road. Despite its sign, it wasn't actually 'North London's Greatest Market', but it was better than nothing.

Despite these additions, there was concern back in the Planning Department for the future of retailing in Holloway. The GLC had designated Wood Green, Ilford, Ealing, Bromley, Kingston and Croydon as the six major strategic shopping centres for outer London, in addition to the West End and the newly-opened Brent Cross out-of-town centre. Lower down in the hierarchy, the Nag's Head was identified as one of twenty-two Strategic Centres. At Wood Green, Haringey Council and Sheppard Robson architects had masterminded a new multi-levelled shopping complex, with pedestrians segregated from traffic by upper walkways, and an enclosed market hall, all connected to multi-storey car parks. When it was finally completed in 1979 it seemed exciting compared to the dangerous roads, grubby buildings and muddy open market in Holloway. Faced with such competition, ambitious plans were drawn up for the Nag's Head, but nothing was immediately forthcoming.

On the leisure front, the Odeon and the Coronet were local flea-pits, while the Rainbow, where I'd seen Bob Marley and the Wailers in July 1977, seemed to hold concerts increasingly rarely. On match days we could hear the roar of the crowd from within the house when Arsenal scored a goal.

The Sobell Centre, with its squash courts and indoor football, was conveniently close, still only four years old and state-of-the-art. The 1930s Hornsey Road Baths were more jaded and sadly under-used, although it was nice to have the big pool almost to oneself. With Greenman Street and Merlin Street Baths still in operation, it wasn't long before the Council decided that the Borough was over-provided with swimming pools.

In the spring of 1978, Susannah York and Ron Moody came to open the newly completed Peter Pan Park in Landseer Road, both having starred in the recent pantomime season at the London Casino Theatre in Old Compton Street. Accompanied by Jean from my office, who'd designed the brick crocodile in the middle, we got to say hello. It was something of a coup for Holloway. At least the Stanley Arms did better as a result, overlooking a new green space, and soon to become one of Tim Martin's first Wetherspoon pubs, renamed J.J. Moons.

I was lucky to have bought the house when I did, as house prices in London continued to rocket. In February 1979, Windsor Road became part of the Axminster Road Housing Action Area. The most negligent landlords were bought out, the Council did up a dozen properties in the street and painted a mural on the flank wall of the house opposite. Three doors along, the Irish family won the pools and had the front of their house clad in fake stone, by a company called Stone Age 2000.

One way or another, the street was 'coming up'. By November 1980 Prebble's were marketing a house in Windsor Road for £47,950, three times what I'd paid just three years before. Retail price inflation wasn't quite so much, but was still 12 per cent in 1977 and 17 per cent in 1979. The 10 per cent pay rises negotiated by NALGO meant that my mortgage repayments got easier.

Best of all, I now had just a ten-minute journey on my bike to the office, and a priceless extra hour every working day. Riding up and down the gritty Holloway Road became my daily ritual, past the ugly, stumpy tower of the Polytechnic of North London where I'd first set foot in August 1972.

A combination of friends and colleagues persuaded me to write a book on Smithfield – Len, Mike and Geoff in the office, Neil and Hannah in the house, and Ros, the girlfriend of Mark, who played French horn in the Hertfordshire Chamber Orchestra. Mark worked for the NatWest Bank's solicitors, Wilde Sapte, in their grim satellite offices in Pentonville Road, and we occasionally met for a slap-up lunch in the beloved Ganpath. Ros worked for the publishers William Heinemann and was an entrée into the world of literature. It seemed like a good project, but how to go about it?

In November 1977 I sent a speculative letter to a number of publishers whom I thought might be suitable and received polite but firm rejections from The Architectural Press in Queen Anne's Gate, Faber & Faber, Longmans, George Allen & Unwin, David & Charles, Oxford University Press and a host of others. 'Good luck elsewhere' was the consistent but not very encouraging message.

However two replies, from Macmillan and Cambridge University Press (CUP), expressed interest in the subject matter, but asked to see sample chapters. CUP said that their usual procedure was to send the complete typescript to one or two specialists in the field who would advise them. Who, after all, would take on a twenty-six-year-old with no track record? Clearly there was no alternative but to write the book first.

In one of several moments of youthful impetuosity and romantic fancy I decided it would be more enjoyable to do this somewhere well away from the distraction of London life. My friends in Kentish Town, Roger and Shantee, decided they wanted to do the same. At my office I asked and received the permission of Denis Browne to carry forward my remaining unused holiday allowance from 1977-78, lump it together with the whole of my four week allocation for 1978-79 and also have a month's unpaid leave.

As a child I'd had family holidays in Wales and Scotland. Apart from a visit one Easter to stay with the grandfather of a school friend in Gorran Haven, I'd never been to Cornwall. In August 1974 I was asked by Richard Cooke to play bassoon in a music festival in North Cornwall. Richard had been a contemporary at university, a choral scholar at King's, and since 1969 he'd been putting on summer concerts in the Parish Church of St Columb Major, where his father, Canon A.G. Cooke, was rector. The town itself had some pretensions, still with a functioning cattle market and plenty of pubs, but with traffic clogging the narrow main street, seemingly in need of a bypass. The assembled orchestra and chamber choir was a clique from Cambridge, Oxford and ex-National Youth Orchestra, enjoying a two-week jamboree of pasties and cream teas, washed down with Redruth's finest Devenish ale, and six concerts thrown in. The only downside was sharing a bedroom at our hosts' cardboard bungalow in Tregoose with the eminent Hugh MacDonald, who snored so badly that I resorted after one sleepless night to hunkering down in the bath. I returned to St Columb in 1977, this time opting for the campsite at Mawgan Porth, no more than a scrubby bit of land above the mini-golf course with a single caravan and a hut with a toilet, but enough room to pitch some tents and the venue for a bacchanalia of late-night drinking, skinny dipping and joke-telling.

The previous April, Neil had asked me to the International Musicians' Seminar (IMS) at Prussia Cove on the South Cornish coast, where Hannah was running the catering and needed help in the kitchen. Elspeth was there too to tune the pianos. The IMS had been founded in 1972 by Hilary Berens, who as a Greenwich resident knew Hannah from her Spread Eagle restaurant. Hilary's brother, Michael, farmed the land above the bay where a cluster of cottages provided the accommodation, and the magnificent Porth-en-Alls mansion housed the tutors, master-classes and communal gatherings. Michael Berens' beautiful and artistic wife Romi sketched the participants.

The three pianists at Prussia Cove, April 1977. From left to right: Peter Pettinger, Ian Brown and Julian Jacobson. (Author's Collection)

The teaching was led by Sándor Végh, the great Hungarian violinist and guru, a friend of Bartok and Kodaly, and a giant of twentieth-century music. He was a man of mesmerising charisma, capable of playing the fiddle like a magician whilst also reducing fragile pupils to tears, and with boorish table manners to boot. The other maestro, Bruno Giurana, was the complete opposite, a perfect and charming gentleman who coaxed a wondrously rich tone from his viola. The youthful Orlando String Quartet were students on the course, and performed the Ravel Quartet in Godolphin House and St Michael's Mount.

More importantly, back in London, I had met Julie, who was studying oboe at the Trinity College of Music and playing in the Hertfordshire Chamber Orchestra. Her father farmed a substantial chunk of land on the north side of Bodmin Moor, ranching cattle and sheep on a grand scale. The land was an amalgamation of many smaller farms but most of the former houses and barns were now ruined, including Ivey Farm, which Julie and Adrian would later refurbish for their own. One small cottage still had its roof and windows, and Julie suggested that Roger, Shantee and I could use it. By May 1978 the official Smithfield Area Plan was done and dusted, the final report written and off at the printers. It was time to go and write the book.

Priest's Hill was no more than a simple, low granite shed, with a Cornish stone roof and Delabole slate floor, a single room with a big draughty fireplace, plus a lean-to galley with a Calor-gas Baby Belling, no running water, no electricity, no bathroom or toilet. After the end of the single-track tarmac lane from St Breward it was then half-a-mile across the open common moorland, skirting the bog and the boulders, to the gate to Priest's Hill field. The house was sheltered by a few stunted sycamore and hawthorn trees and a high earth bank full of foxgloves, but to the north there were open views to the magnificent and dramatic peak of

Priest's Hill cottage (and tent), July 1978. (Author's Collection)

Rough Tor. Below the cottage the juvenile De Lank River burbled through a plantation of firs, and beyond that the long gorse-clad slopes of Garrow rose to the ancient piles of rock on the summit. Our payment, in lieu of rent, was to prune the tree trunks of their lower branches ('brashing' in the local parlance), a rather thankless task. I slept outside in my tent while Roger and Shantee had the bed inside.

We got into a routine of getting up early, writing all morning and then having the rest of the day free for the domestic chores of chopping wood and fetching water, and exploring the moor or the coast, depending on the weather. Some days it rained incessantly, and we were hemmed in by low cloud or fog. I hammered out my manuscript on my noisy Remington Portable, Roger scrawled his own novel in long-hand. Sometimes, after a sunny afternoon at Tregardock or Trebarwith Strand and an evening imbibing Tinners and Hicks Special in the St Kew Inn, we would find that the mist had descended on the moor and we had to grope our way back along the track to Priest's Hill.

We collected our mail from Julie's parents, Peter and Betty, who lived in Fellover, a grand and solid house below St Breward near the River Camel at Tuckingmill. Peter was rarely there, away on the Greek island of Naxos where he loved to sculpt. On my birthday a large cake had arrived from London, baked and posted by a female admirer. 'Someone thinks big o' you,' said the housekeeper.

In retrospect it was odd, only a few months after buying my first house, to go and live somewhere else for three months. But Neil, Hannah and Robin were good house-sitters and kept the home fires burning. By early August I'd finished the manuscript. Neil, Gabriel and I together travelled in my trusty (and rusty) Morris Minor to Bruges to play in the Flanders Festival with Hertfordshire Chamber Orchestra. Then it was down to St Columb to play six

On top of Garrow Tor, August 1978. (Dick Makin)

concerts in the parish church with Richard Cooke and the gang of friends, new and old. Everyone wanted to come and see the hovel where we'd been living, and sample the joys of the Royal Oak at Blisland. On the first Monday in September, after twelve weeks away, it was back to the office in Essex Road. It had been a memorable summer, and Cornwall was now well and truly in my blood.

∽ SOHO AND MAYFAIR ∽

For the two years when I was both living in Kensington and working in Islington, I cycled to and from the office along the full length of Oxford Street, but I rarely diverted south into the grid-plan of streets that was Soho and Mayfair. Ronnie Scott's, the Gay Hussar restaurant in Greek Street, Berwick Street Market, and the irresistible Italian cheese of Alberto Camisa were the only reasons to venture into Soho's sleazy byways. The unspoilt Guinea pub in Bruton Place and the Curzon cinema had been my only ventures into Mayfair property.

In the summer of 1977 Neil had found work as a typist and office dogsbody with Bergström + Boyle Books, a small publisher located in a basement at No. 22 Maddox Street, on the smart Mayfair side of Regent Street. Neil suggested that I should meet Theo Bergström to discuss my ideas for the book about Smithfield. Thus it was one wet evening in October that I descended the steep flight of metal stairs in the narrow front light-well and rang the bell.

The office was an Aladdin's cave of books, manuscripts, piles of paper and photographs, desks and filing cabinets crammed together in a couple of small rooms with uncomfortably low ceilings. Neil, Theo and I adjourned immediately to the Black Lion and French Horn around the corner in Pollen Street, a simple tavern packed with heavy smokers and hardened drinkers.

Theo explained that he was the photographic 'half' of Bergström + Boyle. In the past couple of years they'd been through something of a purple patch producing *Stonehenge* in 1974, which had sold like hot-cakes, and *Hadrian's Wall* in 1975. Having myself recently walked along the Thames, it was a great coincidence that they'd also published in 1975 a source-to-mouth book, *The Thames*, with Theo's moody and atmospheric black-and-white photos and a lyrical commentary by the sculptor Michael Black. Even though it was clear from ordering the drinks that Theo was no great connoisseur of real ale, he'd even recently provided the pictures for *Beer Naturally*, in a co-production with CAMRA and a text by Michael Hardman.

Such was Theo's enthusiasm and spirit of adventure that it didn't take much to interest him in Smithfield, not as a publisher but as photographer. We arranged to meet again so that I could show him round the area. He was as smitten with its potential as I was. For him it came at a good time, as Bergström and Boyle had decided to go their separate ways. Theo needed a 'project' to run alongside his bread-and-butter daily photographic work.

That autumn the office in Maddox Street was vacated and Theo retreated to his studio and flat in Foubert's Place, a small turning off the north end off Carnaby Street, not far from Liberty. Carnaby Street itself, the epitome of 'swinging London' in the '60s, had a more jaded feel by the late '70s. The carriageway had been paved by Westminster Council in gaudy multi-coloured plastic tiles, laid in a jazzy diamond pattern, not soothed by the neon signage and awnings of the boutiques.

Theo's studio was on the first floor of an elegant red-brick Edwardian building, a large open-plan room with a pretty, curved oriel window commanding views southwards down Newburgh Street. To my eyes his routine work, earning a living, appeared far from mundane. Ten years older than me, he moved in different circles. He'd taken cover photos for albums by Bill Wyman and in 1974 for Andy Mackay's *In Search of Eddie Riff*, and done a shoot with Jerry Hall. Theo even had a striking physical resemblance to a clean-cut Bryan Ferry, who'd been Jerry Hall's boyfriend before she took up with Mick Jagger in 1977. Theo had recently been commissioned to do the photography for a series of glossy Octopus cookbooks for Marks & Spencer and he'd set up one side of the studio as a demonstration kitchen for the food hygienists to prepare their perfect dishes. It all seemed rather glamorous.

Theo remarked how he liked to live in the thick of things, and how important it was to be able to buy anything you needed within five minutes of the studio. When a shoot was on, time was money. With Theo as a guide I realised that there was more to Soho than sleaze and clip joints: the Algerian Coffee Shop and Bar Italia in Old Compton Street; Romany's ironmongers and Richards' fishmongers in Brewer Street; the New Piccadilly in Denman Street; Jimmy's in Frith Street; and the Star Café in Great Chapel Street. There was still the tat of the red-light district, the men in grubby raincoats wearing trilby hats (were they customers or plain-clothes police, or both?), but it all seemed less threatening after a good fry-up in a greasy spoon café.

Even with Theo's reputation it didn't prove any easier to find a publisher for the book. On my return from Cornwall I sent the completed text and some sample photos to Macmillan and Cambridge University Press, only to receive replies declining the book. CUP considered it insufficiently academic, and suggested a 'general' publisher; Macmillan thought that it could only justify an unviably small print run.

Fortunately I wrote also to Heinemann, where Ros took up the cudgels. If a sponsor could be found then the figures could be made to work. I wrote a round-robin to dozens of institutions, businesses and City livery companies. I delivered copies of the manuscript to the Museum of London, the Society for the Protection of Ancient Buildings in Great Ormond

Berwick Street Market. (Theo Bergström)

Street, Peter Burman at the Council for Places of Worship, and Hermione Hobhouse at the Victorian Society. The knight in shining armour turned out to be Mr Cullimore of Dewhurst's, part of the Vestey group, who guaranteed to take 1,000 copies, hardback, paid for up-front.

By June 1979 Theo and I had a contract. Now there were frequent visits to Heinemann's genteel offices at No. 15 Queen Street in Mayfair, where the level of civility and decorum matched the address. Ros was editing the manuscript and integrating the illustrations, photos and captions, but the Heinemann director I met was Johnny St John, wonderfully old-school in his three-piece tweed suit and bow tie. I was careful always to wear a jacket and tie too. We went for lunch to the Grosvenor House Hotel, where Heinemann's had an expense account. Some said that they used the smart restaurant almost as a staff canteen. It was a different world from the sticky buns bought from the distinctly un-posh Rendez Vous café in Maddox Street.

We decided to ask Sir John Betjeman to write a foreword and in July I delivered the manuscript to his house in Radnor Walk, Chelsea. Not only had Sir John been Poet Laureate since 1972, but for many years he had lived close to Smithfield Meat Market at No. 43 Cloth Fair, eventually leaving because of the noise from the articulated lorries. Ros suggested that he might even compose something in verse.

Sir John replied saying that he liked the idea of the book, and promised to do something. Sadly, now well into his seventies, he was stricken with Parkinson's Disease and strokes, no longer full of the chuckling gaiety or perky mischief which he'd exuded in *Banana Blush* (recorded in 1974 with Jim Parker's music). It would have been good to talk about the Smithfield he'd known, even to compare notes about Cornwall and Blisland Church, but it wasn't to be. Sir John's writing days were over, verse or no verse. *Smithfield Past and Present*, when it was published early in 1980, never had its foreword.

✎ THE END OF A DECADE ✎

On Thursday 3 May 1979 I went to the office as usual and attended an Offord Road Housing Action Area liaison meeting. I'd done local Council election duties the year before, working as a polling clerk at Hugh Myddelton Primary School, but I hadn't been asked for the general election; perhaps it was better paid and all the old hands wanted to do it. At lunchtime I popped into the Grafton School in Eburne Road to vote for the Ecology Party, currently enjoying a higher profile with the involvement of Jonathon Porritt. The sitting Islington North Labour candidate, Michael O'Halloran, was a shoo-in with the local Irish community.

In the evening I met Elspeth's boyfriend, Mac, and Tim to play cricket in the nets at Finsbury Park. By now Elspeth and Mac were living in one of the roads between Green Lanes and Wightman Road, known as the ladder, and we adjourned to the opulent finery and cut-glass of the Salisbury Hotel to quench our thirst on Charrington's IPA, while Mac the New Zealander stuck to his lager. We talked sport rather than politics.

Back home I sat up for a while with Neil to watch the election results on our fuzzy black-and-white television. Bob McKenzie, Professor of Sociology at the London School of Economics, swung his Swingometer (for the last time as it turned out) and a youthful David Dimbleby fronted the chat. After seeing a downcast Shirley Williams being interviewed by an unsympathetic Robin Day shortly after losing her Hertford and Stevenage seat to the Tories, I went to bed.

It was no surprise that Thatcher won, particularly after all the troubles of the previous winter. There had been a continual sense of dissatisfaction with the government throughout the '70s, whether led by Edward Heath, Harold Wilson, the Lib-Lab pact or 'Sunny' Jim Callaghan. At the time, Margaret Thatcher seemed to be just part of the oscillating pendulum, and probably no more than a temporary aberration who might survive a term if she was lucky. She wasn't even much liked in her own party. Within a few months of the May election VAT had been doubled, and her ratings in public opinion polls plummeted. Besides, even though she now modelled herself as the 'iron lady', who could forget the glossy housewife image of the early '70s when she had been Secretary of State for Education under Edward Heath – 'Margaret Thatcher, Milk Snatcher'?

No one could foresee that Thatcher's unconvincing Churchillian posturing and shallow promise 'to make Britain great again' would be given the unlikely boost of the Falklands War. Who would have bet in 1979 that the left-wing Michael Foot would replace 'Gentleman Jim' as leader of the Labour Party, ahead of Dennis Healey, and that Shirley Williams, David Owen, Roy Jenkins and Bill Rodgers would break away as the 'gang of four' to form the SDP? Socialists assumed that they would bounce back, but Labour hadn't yet penned their manifesto for the next election, described by Gerald Kaufman as 'the longest suicide note in history'. We didn't imagine for a moment in May 1979 that eighteen years of Tory rule lay ahead.

Throughout the 1970s the trade unions had been universally strong. My own union, NALGO, had successfully negotiated substantial pay rises, but nothing like as high as some. The strike at Ford's Dagenham in September 1978 had achieved a 17 per cent pay rise. That winter the Engineering Union asked for 33 per cent and the miners 40 per cent. Industrial action was used almost routinely, sometimes irresponsibly and recklessly. If the three-day-weeks in 1972 and 1973/74 had shown their power, ultimately bringing down the Heath government, then the winter of discontent in 1978/79 was worse, particularly given that retail price inflation was actually considerably lower than in 1974. Although Callaghan was reported as saying 'Crisis, what crisis?', rubbish began to pile up in the streets, *Blue Peter* advised its young viewers on how to keep granny warm during the power cuts, and Hull was dubbed 'Stalingrad' after the ferocity of the blockading lorry drivers.

The leaders of the big unions such as Jack Jones, Lawrence Daly, Jack Dash and Tom Jackson were powerful and domineering figures in the political arena. The fact that most of the main sectors of the economy were nationalised (railways and buses, gas and electricity, coal mines and car factories, telecommunications and the Post Office, British European Airways and British Overseas Airways Corporation, and even Thomas Cook) meant that industrial disputes brought direct confrontation with the government. Free-market entrepreneurs such as Freddie Laker and his Skytrain were regarded as dangerous mavericks. In the end it was a 'no confidence' vote after a defeat on proposals for a referendum on Scottish devolution that brought down Callaghan, but it was probably the straw that broke the camel's back.

Thatcher's election slogan of 'Labour isn't working' was opportune. What fewer people knew about was Keith Joseph's new Centre for Policy Studies, a right-wing think-tank for radical reform plotting to curb the powers of the unions, to privatise almost everything, and give Council-house tenants the right to buy. Although our kitchen stove and hot-water Ascot had been converted to natural gas in 1977, it hadn't occurred to me then that the discovery of North Sea gas and oil would assist so soon in the smashing of the coal industry.

In London the industrial dispute which aroused the most ill-feeling was the Grunwick film-processors' strike in 1977, where police intervention between the pickets and scabs was heavy handed. The Notting Hill riots the previous year, in the stifling August heat, had seen the worst civil unrest for a century, and served to raise the level of tension and the undercurrent of violence. The Metropolitan Police, using or abusing the powers of the 1824 Vagrancy Act, arrested people purely on suspicion, the so-called 'sus laws'. In 1976 55 per cent of arrests for the whole of Britain were made in London, which had only 15 per cent of the population. Of these arrests, 42 per cent were of black people.

In some suburbs of London it was still possible to see notices in windows such as 'Room to let, no Irish or Blacks'. Racial violence was a growing problem, with the National Front and the Anti-Nazi League in militant opposition, coming to a head with the death of Blair Peach in April 1979 at a rally against the National Front in Southall, when he was hit over the head by a police truncheon. Black policemen, and black Members of Parliament, were like hens' teeth.

The potential for police brutality was always a worry at any public rally or demonstration, whether it was the mass gatherings against the Vietnam War in Trafalgar Square and Hyde Park, or smaller protests against Pinochet, Nixon and Kissinger, or Golda Meir.

But although the various global conflicts had their coverage and came to their conclusion, another war, closer to home, afflicted Britain throughout the 1970s. The IRA were particularly active in London, with the bombing of the Post Office Tower in 1971, Earl's Court, the Houses of Parliament and Harrods in 1974, and Oxford Street and the Hilton Hotel in 1975, followed by the Balcombe Street siege. In March 1979 the Shadow Northern Ireland Secretary Airey Neave was blown up in his car while leaving the House of Commons. With Callaghan being seen as 'weak' it probably helped Thatcher win the election, but did nothing to stop Lord Mountbatten being assassinated on his boat in Ireland a few months later.

Less violently, the war of the sexes and the battle for equal rights took centre stage in the '70s. Germaine Greer's *The Female Eunuch*, published in 1970, had lit the touch paper. The 1970 Equal Pay Act had theoretically put women on a better footing and more women were going out to work. The reality was that few were able to progress into senior or managerial jobs beyond the glass ceiling which existed in every sector, both public and private. The emergence of Thatcher was exceptional, and for many feminists, ironic.

The collective magazine *Spare Rib* was started in 1972, edited in their Clerkenwell Close offices by Rosie Boycott and Marsha Rowe, who went on to found Virago Press in 1973. Women were exhorted to give up cooking and typing, and to reject the old adage of 'First you sink into his

Anti-Vietnam war demonstrators. (Mike Bruce)

arms, and then your arms slip into the sink'. WHSmith refused to stock it. The male-dominated establishment press revelled in the sometimes acrimonious debate between the different emerging themes of feminism – socialist, radical, liberal, black and lesbian. Ecologists, environmental activists, CND campaigners and even cyclists were also branded as lunatics or raving lefties. Idealism often became confused with extremism. Tory or Trot seemed to be the choice.

Meanwhile, throughout the 1970s London struggled to throw off the scars of post-war depression. Manufacturing jobs declined by 36 per cent in London (compared to 25 per cent nationally) in the '70s. This decline was not just in the old-fashioned industries in the centre, the East End and docklands, but also affected modern businesses in the suburbs. In November 1979 the Firestone tyre factory in Brentford closed, laying off 1,500 workers, and at the same time Hoover vacated their even more wonderful Art Deco premises on Western Avenue, moving their operations to Cambuslang on the outskirts of Glasgow. Fearful of the vulnerability of London in a Cold War climate to nuclear or conventional attack, Civil Service offices were moved out of London, vehicle licensing to Swansea, income tax to Middlesbrough, and several big insurance companies followed suit. The Location of Offices Bureau, set up in 1964 to deter new offices in London, was still going strong. Only in 1976 did policy switch to trying to support employment and attract jobs back to London. Nor had the financial sector, still hide-bound by restrictions and old-school-tie traditions, yet risen to replace the jobs of declining industry. The City indeed feared competition from Frankfurt, Paris, Tokyo and New York. For tens of thousands of Londoners, the 'Super Seventies' were far from super.

It was also a time of enormous social upheaval in London. With the loss of traditional jobs, continuing poor housing conditions and environmental degradation, many long-suffering people were only too keen to leave London for Milton Keynes or the expanding towns in

Marsham Street, 1977.
(English Heritage)

Essex, Kent and Hertfordshire. In the London Borough of Islington, at least two-thirds of the residents who'd been there in 1971 had left or died by 1981 (according to Jerry White). This massive turnover was also exacerbated by the ambitious municipal housing programme, most of which came to a shuddering halt after 1979 when Thatcher wielded the axe on social programmes and public spending.

London's population declined in the '70s to its lowest since 1900. *The Good Life* might have been a successful television comedy series set in 1975 Surbiton, but also reflected middle-class aspirations.

The architectural legacy in London from the 1970s is considerable, but very patchy in quality. Now that the whole decade is eligible, under the thirty-year rule for listing buildings, it is proving hard to find many candidates which do not draw incredulity from some quarters. Several of the more prestigious public housing schemes such as the Marquess and Market Road Estates in Islington have not survived. Similarly, in the City of London many 1970s office buildings have already disappeared in the never-ending renewal of fabric.

The true legacy is perhaps one of ideas and styles. The 1970s saw the culmination and end of Brutalism, with the completion of mega-projects such as the National Theatre, the Barbican and the Brunswick Centre, all designed in the '60s. Sadly, some of the worst monsters such as Basil Spence's top-heavy Home Office in Petty France, looming over St James's Park, or Elsom Pack Roberts' blocks in Victoria Street near Westminster Cathedral, tarnish the reputation of the whole decade. Worst of all were the Aylesbury and Heygate Estates in Southwark. At least we can be thankful that the Marsham Street slabs were eventually demolished.

The new 'kid on the block' was Hi-Tech. When Richard Rogers' and Renzo Piano's Pompidou Centre opened in Paris in 1977, it turned the architectural world upside-down or, more accurately, inside-out. In London, Michael Hopkins' house in Hampstead, Norman Foster's IBM warehouse at Greenford and Aukett's factory for Landis & Gyr provided more minimalist and elegant versions of Hi-Tech.

Another alternative to Brutalism emerged with the spirit of contextualism, not only the ubiquitous low-rise brick-skinned public housing, but also the use of homely vernacular on a monumental scale, as at Hillingdon's new Civic Centre at Uxbridge. Further reaction saw the birth of post-modernism, the age of pluralism and structural expressionism, and the first of a wave of new buildings constructed behind retained façades.

The conservation movement took heart from the triumphs at Covent Garden and Spitalfields, although their battles were far from over. The Civic Trust, guided by Gordon Mitchell at the Wirksworth project, promoted community-led conservation as an engine for urban regeneration. The Smithfield Plan provided a new vision for Clerkenwell and a blueprint for the inner city. In 1979 the Thirties Society was formed (later re-named the Twentieth Century Society), sadly not in time to save the Firestone Building. The Heritage of London Trust was set up to give grants to help the repair historic structures and artefacts. Some things did get better in the 1970s.

Other innovations, which seemed like progress at the time, are more debatable. New self-service supermarkets offered reliable and good-value food (and jobs for checkout girls and shelf stackers), and nobody thought much about the threat to local shops. New chains like Block & Quayle (B&Q) grew from one outlet in 1969 to twenty-six by 1979, including several in London suburbs, offering cheap kitchen units and DIY products. Although some people worried that we might become the 51st state of America, few could imagine the corporate world of Primark, Starbucks or Amazon which lay ahead.

It is possible to look back at the '70s with a variety of emotions – nostalgia, regret, anger or laughter. While some of its most extreme characters such as Sid Vicious didn't make it to the end of the decade, others subsequently mellowed. Johnny Rotten, after all, ended up advertising Country Life butter, a different form of decadence.

A recent return visit to Harrow, the first time since I'd left in 1974, was a sobering experience. Passing through the suburbs of Kenton and Kingsbury, I was the only cyclist on roads choked with traffic. In some streets every front garden had been paved for car parking. Huge queues of vehicles waited to get into sprawling superstores. In Wealdstone, the bypass had been built and a new mosque now rivalled the Civic Centre on the opposite side of the road. The Railway Hotel had been replaced by a dull block of flats, called Moon House. Harrow-on-the-Hill still had a genteel air, but too genteel. The North Star public house was now a private house and the King's Head Hotel had been converted to flats. No. 65 Welldon Crescent, where I'd briefly lodged in 1973, had been demolished with its neighbours for Bradbury Court sheltered housing. Returning through Hendon, the White Bear was now revamped as Fernandez Grill Bar, and the cinema was a Virgin Active Health Club. It seemed a strange coincidence that, after increasing her majority as MP for Finchley, Thatcher's first public speech as Prime Minister in May 1979 was made in the old Hendon Town Hall in The Burroughs, just yards from where I'd first landed in London.

Today, Queen's Gate Terrace in Kensington is uniformly smart. Waitrose in Gloucester Road is now Partridges of Kensington, posher and pricier. The Harrington is renamed the Prince Regent. The single-bar metal gate in St Alban's Grove, on which we use to practise our tightrope skills returning from the Builders' Arms, has wisely been removed. You can now cycle, on designated paths, in Hyde Park and Kensington Gardens. One route, called Policeman's Walk, even takes you past the scene of my arrest.

Looking back, life in the 1970s was very different; it was a world without mobile phones, Blackberries, email, texts, blogs, Twitter, Facebook, satnav, GPS, compact discs, digital cameras and late-night television. There were fewer gadgets in the home and less tyrannical jargon in the office, mercifully unencumbered by concepts of 360-degree appraisals or hot-desking. It was a different planet; life on Mars indeed.

One might also argue that there was less cynicism and greater naivety in the '70s, more optimism that the world could be changed for the better. Society was as yet untarnished by Thatcherite values that the only things worth having were those you could pay for, or by the New Labour fad for targets and box-ticking. We had not yet become, as Andrew Marr was later to say, Thatcher's children.

For me, the 1970s in London were pure serendipity, a decade of discovery and diversity, developing an interest and landing a job in the built environment, performing a large amount of the classical orchestral repertoire, writing a book, buying a house, and meeting and making a lot of new friends, almost none of whom, I'm delighted to say, went on to run the country. I was best man at a couple of weddings, but remained a bachelor. Aged twenty-eight in 1979, my course was set. Ahead lay a multi-stranded career, or perhaps more honestly a jack-of-all-trades and master-of-none. And by then, I knew there was nowhere better for that than London.

Looking east from The Monument, 1974. (Richard Brockman)